Leckie ✕ **Leckie**

Scotland's leading educational publishers

D1388255

CfE Higher
ENGLISH
GRADE A BOOSTER

CfE Higher ENGLISH
GRADE A BOOSTER

David Cockburn

001/05052015

10 9 8 7 6 5 4 3 2 1

ISBN 9780007589012

Published by
Leckie & Leckie Ltd
An imprint of HarperCollins*Publishers*
Westerhill Road, Bishopbriggs, Glasgow, G64 2QT
T: 0844 576 8126   F: 0844 576 8131
leckieandleckie@harpercollins.co.uk
www.leckieandleckie.co.uk

Publisher: Fiona Burns
Project manager: Craig Balfour

Special thanks to
Roda Morrison (copy edit)
Helen Bleck (proofread)
Keren McGill (editorial)
Jouve (layout)
Ink Tank (cover)

Printed in Italy by Grafica Veneta S.p.A.

A CIP Catalogue record for this book is available from the British Library.

Acknowledgements
Extracts from 'Cutting down a tree is worse than fox hunting' by Janice Turner on pages 13–14 and 15–16, and 'Addicted to Shopping' by Carol Midgley on pages 44–45 published in The Times and reproduced by permission of The Times; questions from SQA exams on pages 14, 16, 18, 31, 36, 79 and 80 reproduced by permission of Scottish Qualifications Authority; extract from 'Don't be beguiled by Orwell: using plain and clear language is not always a moral virtue' by Ed Smith on page 18 published in the New Statesman and reproduced by permission of the New Statesman; two extracts from 'Why I Write', and extracts from 'A Hanging', and 'Shooting an Elephant' by George Orwell on pages 23, 153, 26 and 27 respectively reproduced by permission of A.M Heath Literary Agents; extract from *The Pure Heart* by Susan Hill on page 24 reproduced by permission of Vintage; extract from *The Body In Question* by Jonathan Miller on page 29 published by Random House and reproduced by permission of David Higham Associates; extract from 'Is it OK to fly?' by Leo Hickman on page 30 published in The Guardian and reproduced by permission of Guardian News and Media; extract from 'Despite Google, we still need good libraries' by George Kerevan on page 36 published in The Scotsman and reproduced by permission of The Scotsman; extracts from 'In praise of catwomen' by Rebecca McQuillan on page 39 and 'It's a bigger killer than heroin. Why should it be cheap?' by Ian Bell on page 42, published in The Herald and reproduced by permission of The Herald; extract from *Shakespeare* by Bill Bryson on page 43 reproduced by permission of HarperCollins Publishers; extracts from *The Cone-Gatherers* on pages 55 and 83–85, and *Under the Skin* by Michael Faber on page 56 reproduced by permission of Canongate Books; extract from *A Streetcar Named Desire* by Tennessee Williams on pages 61–62 reproduced by permission of Sheil Land Associates Ltd; extract from *Death of a Salesman* on pages 65–67 and *View from the Bridge* on page 71 by Arthur Miller reproduced by permission of The Wylie Agency (UK) Ltd; extract from *Men Should Weep* by Ena Lamont Stewart on pages 74–76 reproduced by permission of Alan Brodie representation; 'Havisham' by Carol Ann Duffy on page 99 reproduced by permission of the author c/o Rogers Coleridge & White Ltd; 'An Autumn Day' by Sorley MacLean on pages 106–107 and 'My Rival's House' by Liz Lochhead on pages 110–111 reproduced by permission of Birlinn Ltd; 'Mr Bleaney' by Philip Larkin on pages 127–128 reproduced by permission of Faber & Faber; 'Waiting Room' by Moira Andrew on page 135 reproduced by permission of Moira Andrew; extract from 'Regeneration' by Pat Barker reproduced by permission of Penguin; extract from *The Crystal Bucket* by Clive James reproduced by permission of United Agents

From the author: *I owe and incalculable debt to several people: to Ina and Joe Barclay, my in-laws, a true lady and a perfect gentleman, both sadly now departed, for the enormous encouragement and joy and inspiration they gave me; to Meg and Willie Cockburn, whose passion for language inspired me at a young age; to the team at Leckie, whose talents know no bounds; and most importantly to Kevin Cockburn without whom this book would never have been written.*

Whilst every effort has been made to trace the copyright holders, in cases where this has been unsuccessful, or if any have inadvertently been overlooked, the Publishers would gladly receive any information enabling them to rectify any error or omission at the first opportunity.

Contents

Introduction

Introduction

It is often said that Higher English is one of the easiest Highers to pass and one of the most difficult in which to excel. Certainly it's true that considerably more pupils score 'A' grades in Physics and French than they do in English. This book is intended to try to improve performance, especially yours, in Higher English.

You already know that it isn't enough just to pass Higher English; you need to do well and, to do well, you need to develop your linguistic, literary and critical skills. This is no mean feat, but rest assured that this book will give you all the help you require in order to succeed and to boost your grade.

For the Reading for Understanding, Analysis and Evaluation (RUAE) paper, you will learn how to analyse sentence structure and how it can be manipulated to create various effects; you will also learn about word choice, tone, punctuation, paragraph linkage, imagery and many other literary and linguistic devices.

To excel in the Critical Reading paper, you will learn how to approach and study the various literary genres (drama, fiction, non-fiction and poetry) and how to prepare texts for the examination. You will learn about narrative structure, characterisation, symbolism, and setting, rhythm, rhyme: all important literary techniques that will help you understand, analyse and evaluate all the texts that you'll be studying this year.

Rest assured, you will also be shown how to answer the Scottish text questions and how to write a critical essay.

You will, then, learn everything you need to know about the skills of linguistic and literary analysis in order to succeed effectively in the course and in the external assessments.

But please bear in mind that English doesn't really divide into neat segments called Reading for Understanding, Analysis and Evaluation on the one hand and Critical Reading in the other. Your approach to the subject should be holistic –the very reading techniques that you learn to excel at in the RUAE paper overlap with the techniques you need to analyse literature. That is, everything you learn in this book for Reading for UAE will help you in your approach, especially to your analysis of drama and fiction. Knowledge of sentence structure will also help you in your analysis of poetry.

Reading and writing are actually two sides of the same coin: the more you build your skills in reading analytically and evaluatively, the better you will write. As you gain skills in writing, you develop even further your skills in reading. It's an upward spiral!

Each chapter of this book will provide you with two important elements:

- the knowledge, skills and techniques you need;
- worked examples employing those skills and techniques;

But first of all, let's be clear about all that is involved in the Higher English course and its related internal and external assessments.

The Higher course and the assessments

Higher English involves two separate but related features: the course itself and the assessments, both internal and external.

Course arrangements

The Higher English course is made up of two mandatory units:

(a) Analysis and Evaluation Unit;
(b) Creation and Production Unit.

Both units (a) and (b) above include the four language skills of listening, talking, reading and writing.

Both units can be delivered by your teacher in a number of different ways but, however the course is approached, your teacher must cover and assess certain skills, such as:

(a) for Analysis and Evaluation, you must have knowledge and understanding of and be assessed in the skills of

- listening and reading within the contexts of literature, language and media; and
- analysis and evaluation of detailed and complex texts, both literary and non-literary.

(b) for Creation and Production, you must develop and be assessed in

- talking and writing skills in a wide range of contexts; and
- skills of creating and producing detailed and complex texts, both written and oral.

Both units are internally assessed, either unit-by-unit or by combined assessments which involve both units at the same time.

To gain the award of the course, you must pass all of the Unit internal assessments as well as the external assessment.

External assessment

The external assessment involves an examination as well as a submitted portfolio, as set out below:

Paper 1 (Reading for Understanding, Analysis and Evaluation), lasting 1 hour and 30 minutes; and

Paper 2 (Critical Reading), lasting 1 hour and 30 minutes.

The question paper will have two sections:

Section 1

Application of reading skills (understanding, analysis
and evaluation) of two non-fiction texts — 30 marks

Section 2

There are two parts to this section:

Part 1 – one Scottish text from a list of specified
texts (drama, prose, poetry), candidates
to answer questions — 20 marks

Part 2 – one critical essay (drama, prose,
poetry, language, media) — 20 marks

Total (both sections) — **70 marks**

Externally assessed portfolio

Two written texts that address the main
language purposes (discursive writing as
well as creative writing) — 30 marks

Overall total — **100 marks**

Section 1: Reading for Understanding, Analysis and Evaluation

Reading for Understanding, Analysis and Evaluation

This *Grade 'A' Booster*, as the name suggests, is intended not just to help you pass Higher English, but to help you do well, to enable you to achieve the highest grade possible. To manage that, you need to know as much as possible about how the English language works.

Such knowledge about language will also enable you to write more accurately and grammatically. It is important to remember that success in all your subjects depends on your ability to read with care and understanding as well as on your ability to write accurately, grammatically and coherently. Therefore, knowledge about how language works is essential.

To increase your knowledge and understanding of the ways in which our language works, you are best to establish good habits, right now. Since the passages for the RUAE paper are often taken from quality newspapers and magazines, it would be to your advantage to establish a habit of reading articles from such sources weekly. Don't read everything! Choose, say, one article a week, one that captures your interest or, better still, widens your interest throughout your Higher course. As you practise such reading, you'll get used to the language features and the vocabulary, which you should note to ensure you widen yours! Use a notebook to record arresting sentences, phrases and individual words.

Furthermore, when it comes to talking skills, understanding your language will enable you to become more articulate, increasing your ability to express orally your thoughts and feelings more clearly.

The Reading for Understanding, Analysis and Evaluation (RUAE) paper

If you examine carefully the RUAE paper, you will see that there are various question types that keep recurring, such as questions about sentence structure, word choice, imagery, link sentences and so on. As we study each of these question types in this section, you will be presented with the language skills and any relevant grammatical knowledge that you need to help you answer the question effectively and accurately.

Question types

We can classify the question types into four main categories:

1. Questions about understanding;

2. Questions that ask you to analyse;

3. Questions that ask you to evaluate;

4. Questions on both passages.

> **Important point !**
>
> Please also remember that, although we are dealing with the RUAE paper at this point, everything you learn here about sentence structure will help you when it comes to the analysis of drama, fiction, non-fiction and poetry.

In this section, we will examine each type of question, mostly using the following approach:

• first, an explanation of the question type;

• second, a procedure setting out how to answer the question;

• third, a worked example.

1. Questions about understanding

When answering questions about understanding, you must always use your own words.

Such questions can be identified by words such as:

• 'Identify', which indicates that you should be brief, naming the relevant points, but always using your own words;

• 'Explain' or 'In what way(s)', both of which instruct you to make clear the ways in which aspects of the writer's ideas relate to one another or contribute to his or her line of thought. Again, you must use your own words.

It is very important to read the question carefully, paying particular attention to the task. The RUAE paper is a test of reading skills, and if you don't read the question properly, then you can't expect to succeed.

Procedure

Use the following procedure in all cases:

(a) Read the question carefully and note the **task**.

(b) Go to the text and underline the expression(s) which contain the answer.

(c) Convert that expression as far as you can into your own words – don't waste time trying to translate the expression, just make sure you convey the general idea or gist – this is key to answering these types of question.

(d) Check that you have met the demands of the task.

Worked example

This example is taken from the specimen paper for Higher English. The writer of this passage considers the value of trees. In the article, the writer has been explaining that commercial developers, backed by government, destroy trees in order to make way for new roads and industrial estates. The writer argues, though, that many ordinary folk, unlike officialdom and councils, love trees.

Read the following extract carefully:

Yet it is astonishing, given how much people love them — planting them to mark special moments or honour dead loved ones, measuring their lives by their seasonal changes — that officialdom loathes trees. Insurance companies fretting about subsidence would rather you took them all down just in case. Councils detest them, employing municipal butchers to hack away at whole groves. Embarrassed stumps with a couple of twigs are all that remain.

It's a wonder any tree survives a health and safety audit. One City Council tried to remove a whole row of horsechestnuts because conkers fell on cars

(continued)

and children might slip on leaves. Our local primary school cut down a fine tree beneath which generations of children had played, because the new head deemed its twigs and leaves too messy. A posh gardener once suggested we cut down most of our trees and start again with fresh, more groovy varieties. This misunderstood the very point: trees are the antithesis of fickle fashion. But some crass homeowners can't bear the fluff-balls from plane trees messing up their hall carpet or the lime sap puking down on their shiny car bonnets. Neater to reach for the axe. Maybe garden centres should start selling plastic ones: say goodbye to autumnal hell.

Visiting Burma, I learnt that its teak forests were flogged off to China by the generals, who were desperate for quick cash, like a beautiful girl being forced to sell her hair. Iceland is barren because Vikings cut them all down in a year and Peru is logging away its resources.

Our country's trees will tumble to make way for the machines of progress. But for how much economic growth is it worth mowing down a wood? Trees are beyond priceless: they are our history inscribed in the natural world. Which rich men, planting beautiful orchards to their own glorious memory, have always known.

Adapted from an article in *The Times*, January 2013

Q Identify four reasons given in these lines for cutting down trees. You should use your own words as far as possible. (4 marks)

You **must** use your own words – if you quote then you will score no marks and no-one can afford to throw away 4 marks.

There are several reasons:

- trees are felled because there is a worry that they can help cause land to sink, thus causing buildings to shift dangerously or collapse;
- trees can damage vehicles;

- they can cause young people to injure themselves;
- in autumn they can cause an unsightly mess;
- some trees are felled because they are regarded as unfashionable – to be replaced by a more trendy variety;
- there is profit to be made by selling off trees;
- some are transformed to timber for mercantile purposes;
- many are felled for the sake of development.

You have only to select four reasons to gain the 4 marks, but make sure you follow the (a)–(d) procedure above. You can answer in continuous prose or in bullet points.

Here is an example of a good answer:

The four reasons are that (a) trees are felled because there is a worry that they could cause the land to sink and therefore houses to collapse; (b) councils want rid of trees that can harm vehicles when their leaves, twigs and even sap fall onto them; (c) trees are felled for the profit obtained when selling the timber; and (d) some trees are even cut down to be replaced by more trendy, up-to-date versions.

Worked example

The other type of understanding question uses the expressions 'Explain' or 'In what way(s)'. Read the extract that follows, then we'll examine such a question to see how it should be answered:

And this week, reading how some protesters had been arrested trying to prevent ancient woodland being destroyed to make way for a three-mile link road to Hastings, I thought: yes, I'd go to prison for a tree. Indeed, the protesters who are digging tunnels in the mud and standing before the diggers are not "eco-warriors" or "hippies". Among them are young families, retired folk and ordinary dog-walkers. "Local grandmothers", it was reported, came to swing in giant hammocks strung between the 400-year-old oaks.

(continued)

But this is their last stand. They can only slow the developers. By March the trees will be felled. Local people have fought for 20 years to save them, but they are on the wrong side of what the government is determined to market as progress, however short-term and dubious the economic benefits. The Chancellor of the Exchequer gave £56·8 million of government money for this very road, which will fill up with extra traffic, as new roads do, and lead in time to a spanking new industrial estate, although Hastings town already has plenty of boarded-up premises from which to trade.

Q According to the writer, in what ways are the protesters different from how we might expect them to be? (2 marks)

Remember that the expressions 'Explain' and 'In what way(s)' demand you have to make clear any related ideas, as set out by the writer. This is a question about the relationship of ideas.

In the passage, the writer states: 'Indeed, the protesters who are digging tunnels in the mud and standing before the diggers are not "eco-warriors" or "hippies". Among them are young families, retired folk and ordinary dog-walkers. "Local grandmothers", it was reported, came to swing in giant hammocks strung between the 400-year-old oaks.' In these sentences the writer makes clear her view about (a) what kind of people the protesters are not, then (b) what kind of people they in fact are.

A good answer, then, might be:

we expect protesters to be ardent activists dedicated to the conservation of the

Important point

Candidates are let down badly in Higher English because their vocabulary is so limited. Spend the entire year building up your vocabulary. Buy yourself an A5 notebook (as well as a quality newspaper every week) and note down any unfamiliar words you come across – look up the meaning in the dictionary or online and note it in your notebook. Get used to doing this regularly. Increase your vocabulary from a few hundred words to thousands! And check how to spell the words at the same time. The more extensive your vocabulary, the easier it will be for you to articulate your thoughts and ideas.

environment ('eco-warriors') and people who reject conformist societal attitudes in favour of unconventional lifestyles ('hippies') (1 mark), whereas in reality they are just ordinary people of all ages from a representative range of society (1 mark).

2. Questions that ask you to analyse

Such questions are about analysing the ways in which language features shape meaning and help portray the ideas of the passage. The features can include **word choice**, **imagery**, **sentence structure**, **punctuation** and **tone**.

As always, there will be a task set and you **must** pay attention to the task. Too many candidates struggle to gain marks in word-choice questions, for example, because they do not relate the connotations of the chosen word to the task set.

Procedure

Follow this procedure if the question is about, say, **imagery**:

(a) Read the question carefully, paying particular attention to the **task set**.

(b) Pick out the appropriate image from the passage and consider the literal meaning.

(c) Then show how the literal meaning contributes by means of the figurative meaning to the task set.

(d) Finally, use the formula 'Just as x is the case, so the image conveys ...' to structure your answer. This is explained on the next page.

Worked example

Here is an example of an analysis question from the specimen paper. You need to refer again to the first extract above.

> **Q** By referring to at least one example, analyse how the writer's use of imagery emphasises her opposition to cutting down trees. (2 marks)

First of all, you need to recognise the relevant images, but remember that merely naming the image won't attract any marks. The task is to make a perceptive comment on how the image emphasises her opposition to cutting down trees. It is useful and effective, when answering such questions, to use the 'just as ... so ...' formula: for example, take the sentence 'Councils detest them, employing municipal butchers to hack away at whole groves.' Clearly, once you have identified 'butchers' as an image, you have to think of the connotations of the word – what is it that butchers do? Unlike surgeons, they carve up a dead animal into large chunks, though there is also the suggestion that their work is fairly violent and wholesale.

A good answer, then, using the formula above, might be:

She emphasises her opposition to tree-cutting by her use of the image 'butchers'; just as a butcher carves up an animal into large pieces in a violent and crude way (1 mark), so municipal workers chop at trees in a similar brutish manner (1 mark).

Worked example

Now we'll attempt a more challenging question about **word choice**. The following is an extract from an essay by Ed Smith, a columnist with *The New Statesman*, published in February 2013. The essay is about the ways in which politicians can use the language of persuasion in an effort to gain our support:

There is an irony about George Orwell's essay *Politics and the English Language*. Orwell argues that the sins of obfuscation and euphemism followed inevitably from the brutalities of his political era (the 1930s and 1940s). In the age of the atom bomb and the Gulag, politicians reached for words that hid unpalatable truths. By contrast, our era of vague political muddle and unclear dividing lines has inspired a snappy, gritty style of political language: the no-nonsense, evidence-backed, bullet-pointed road to nowhere.

Q Analyse the way in which the writer uses word choice to express his disapproval of our era of political language. (3 marks)

Note the task: it concerns the writer's disapproval of today's political *language*, therefore we must concentrate on the words he uses to describe the language of our politicians. We need to examine expressions such as *snappy, gritty style of political language* and *the no-nonsense, evidence-backed, bullet-pointed road to nowhere.*

Comment

Given that politics is a serious matter, for the writer to refer to the language used by politicians as 'snappy' and 'gritty' is clearly disapproving: 'snappy' can suggest language which is irritable and grumpy, but it could also suggest something snazzy and superficially trendy, like a cheap tie, thus expressing a tone which is unfavourable and contemptuous; 'gritty', in this context, is also a pejorative term, suggesting language which is unnecessarily harsh and coarse, lacking in fluency and eloquence. Today's political language, according to the writer, is superficial and curt, underdeveloped and lacking in style, thus expressing his disapproval. (Such a developed point would gain all 3 marks.)

> **Important point**
>
> The word 'pejorative' suggests using a word in an insulting or degrading way.

In the expression that follows – *the no-nonsense, evidence-backed, bullet-pointed road to nowhere* – the phrase *road to nowhere* makes clear his disapproval of prose which is *no-nonsense, evidence-backed* and *bullet-pointed*. The term *no-nonsense* suggests language which is supposed to appeal because of its directness, but which, in fact, is disarmingly over-simplified; *evidence-backed* again is supposed to appeal because there is the suggestion of reliability, but which is dishonest and beguiling because it only affects plainness and merely appears uncomplicated; the term *bullet-pointed* again suggests straightforward simplicity, whereas in fact such lists tend to lack development and are only superficially attractive.

> **Important point**
>
> Do you know the meaning of the words 'obfuscation' and 'euphemism'? If not, did you look them up and note them in your vocabulary notebook? And what about 'beguiling' and 'pejorative'?

Sentence structure

Perhaps the questions that cause the greatest anxiety are questions about sentence structure. The question is likely to ask about features of language, of which sentence structure is one. For example, 'Analyse how the writer's use of language emphasises …'

Let's concentrate to begin with on sentence structure as a feature of language.

When it comes to examining the ways in which a given sentence is structured, there are various things to look out for; in particular you have to know about various structural techniques, such as a writer's use of:

(a) subordination/inversion;

(b) lists (both polysyndetic and asyndetic)/tricolon;

(c) adverbs or adverbial phrases at the beginning of sentences;

(d) a long sentence followed by a short one;

(e) unusual word groups/binaries;

(f) interrogatives/questions; imperatives/commands; punctuation; parenthesis; minor sentences;

(g) a sudden switch in tense, particularly to the present tense;

(h) also look out for repetition in any of the above.

Although it is important to be able to identify these various kinds of sentence structure, it is also even more important to be able to analyse their various effects. Very often the effect of many of these structural devices is to produce climax, drawing attention to/stressing the main point by placing it at the end of a sentence or clause or list.

You need to read the relevant piece of text very carefully, then decide which of the above sentence structure techniques apply. Once you have done that, then make sure that you relate your analysis of the sentence structure to the task as outlined in the question.

Let's examine the effects of each type of sentence structure in turn:

(a) subordination/inversion

Subordination is the name we give to the sentence structure where the main clause comes at the end. When a writer places the subordinate clause at the beginning of a sentence, he or she is in effect altering the 'normal' order of that sentence. The writer is inverting the sentence.

Worked example

The following amended sentence is taken from a passage where the author argues that popular culture (such as video games) can be as valuable for young people's mental development as traditional reading.

Read and note the sentence carefully:

——— **Subordinate clause** ———   ——— **Main clause** ———
Where most critics allege a dumbing down, I see a progressive story.

What is the effect of altering 'normal' word order?

English is a word-ordered language: alter the order of words in a sentence and you alter the meaning. In the above example, the normal word order would be 'I see a progressive story where most critics allege a dumbing down'. But in the above case the structure of the sentence has been inverted by placing the main clause (the author's view) at the end, thus emphasising it – giving it added weight.

On the other hand, sometimes inversion creates a form of climax, drawing attention to the main clause which comes at the end.

Placing the subordinate clause at the beginning of a sentence can have yet another effect: it can suggest formal writing.

(b) lists

Often when you are asked about sentence structure, the answer has to do with lists, of which there are various kinds:

(i) polysyndetic lists, where there are conjunctions between each item;

(ii) asyndetic lists, where the list has no conjunctions;

21

(iii) anaphoric lists (anaphora), where the first few words of clauses/sentences are repeated – this kind of list is sometimes referred to as a list in parallel structure; and

(iv) tricolon – with three items in the list, where usually the penultimate and ultimate items are linked by a conjunction, and where the effect is both pleasing and persuasive.

(i) polysyndetic lists – such lists are recognisable by the use of conjunctions (usually 'and' or 'or') between each item. The writer Ernest Hemingway (1899–1961) was renowned for his use – some would say overuse – of polysyndeton.

The effect of a polysyndetic list is usually to highlight individually each item in the list, building to a final climax, but creating the impression that the items are significant in themselves, yet causally linked. These lists often culminate in or draw attention to the final item.

Worked example

Let's see how knowledge of lists can help with the analysis of poetry. The following example is the polysyndetic list at the beginning of *Sonnet 65* by Shakespeare. In this case, Shakespeare employs the conjunction 'nor':

Since brass, nor stone, nor earth, nor boundless sea,

But sad mortality o'ersways their power

In this example, each item is individually stressed, drawing attention to its importance, culminating in the idea that everything, no matter what, perishes and dies ('sad mortality o'ersways their power').

Also note that within the list there is climax: it begins with something small and recognisable – 'brass' – building up through larger and larger items, until 'boundless sea', which seems limitless. The effect is to stress further the power of mortality – even the massive sea will one day be destroyed. Notice also the repetition of the word 'nor', further drawing attention to the idea that everything perishes. But note also the conjunction 'but' leading to the sonnet's ultimate climax that 'mortality' is the final, most powerful force.

(ii) asyndetic lists – such lists are easily recognisable by the lack of conjunctions between the items. The effect is to indicate the range and extent and the significance of the items in the list, and also sometimes to draw attention to the importance of the final item by means of climax.

Worked example

In the following extract from his essay, *Why I Write*, George Orwell explains that one of the motives for writing is 'sheer egoism' – 'the desire to seem clever, to be talked about, to be remembered after death':

> Writers share this characteristic with scientists, artists, politicians, lawyers, soldiers, successful businessmen – in short, with the whole top crust of humanity.

The list – 'scientists, artists, politicians, lawyers, soldiers, successful businessmen' – is clearly asyndetic, since there are no conjunctions. The effect is to give the range and extent of the 'top crust', who share egoism as a motive or characteristic of ambitious, successful individuals. Indeed, there is a need for such an illustrative list in order to clarify the kind of people Orwell is talking about.

There is also a hint of climax in that the final item is made up of two polysyllabic words instead of just one word.

(iii) lists using anaphora/parallel structure – such repetition is where there is repetition of clauses or phrases or words. Parallel structure is often referred to simply as repetition, but also, more technically, as **anaphora**, the effects of which are almost always emphatic.

Worked example

In the following example from Chapter 65 of *The Pure in Heart* by Susan Hill, the narrator is explaining that there were no new developments concerning the disappearance of the schoolboy:

> There was no news, no trace, no sign.

You cannot help noticing the repetition of 'no' in front of each noun.

In this example, repetition emphasises, draws attention to, the negative, stressing the fact that there has been no news at all.

(iv) tricolon – tricolon is a special form of list, though it is much, much more common than you would imagine. Once you are aware of it, you'll spot its use on so many occasions.

Tricolon is special because, as the name suggests, there are always three items in such a list. It can also be a combination of lists, each with three items. The effect is mostly always rhetorical, a slightly theatrical way of attracting the reader's attention to persuade him/her to the writer's point of view. It is therefore a device much loved and used by politicians!

Worked example

The most famous example, perhaps, of tricolon is the sentence structure of the American Declaration of Independence. The first article under the American Declaration of the Rights and Duties of Man states:

> Article I. Every human being has <u>the right to life</u>, <u>liberty</u> and <u>the security of his person</u>.

And note its use in this famous sentence:

> We hold these truths to be self-evident, <u>that all men are created equal</u>, <u>that they are endowed by their Creator with certain unalienable Rights</u>, <u>that among these are Life, Liberty and the pursuit of Happiness</u>.

Right away you can detect the use of tricolon – in Article I the three items are (i) the right to life; (ii) liberty; and (iii) the security of the person. Each item is the object of the verb 'has' and the three listed in this way form the tricolon.

In the second example above, there are overall three items in the list – (a) that all men are created equal; (b) that they are endowed by their Creator with certain unalienable rights; and (c) that among these are Life, Liberty and the pursuit of Happiness.

But the observant will also have noticed that the third item is also a tricolon, having three items within it – (i) Life; (ii) Liberty; and (iii) the pursuit of Happiness.

What is so special about the effect of tricolon? It is, as we have already noted, a rhetorical device, much adopted by orators such as Abraham Lincoln, Martin Luther King, Winston Churchill and Barack Obama. It is effective orally because of the rhythm that the speaker can use and emphasise by building up to the final item, which is usually longer, more intense and more conclusive than the previous two (there – we've just used a tricolon!). The tricolon should repeat certain phrases, as in (a), (b) and (c) above.

When you come across a tricolon, look for:

- the three items that form the tricolon;
- the identifiable use of rhythm;
- the repetition of certain phrases, or phrases that follow a common verb;
- the use of emphasis, especially of the final item;
- the increasing length of the items, helping to construct the climactic nature of the final item;
- the conclusive, even dramatic, nature of the final item;
- the attention that the tricolon brings to meaning.

(c) adverbs or adverbial phrases at the beginning of sentences

The placing of adverbs or adverbial phrases at the beginning of sentences is commoner than you might think. Like inversion, this device involves breaking the normal word order of a sentence, though this time to put a word or phrase at the beginning of the sentence for emphasis.

Worked example

Read the following sentence from Orwell's *A Hanging*:

> Suddenly, when we had gone ten yards, the procession stopped short without any order or warning.

You can see immediately that he has disturbed the normal word order, which would be:

> The procession stopped short suddenly without any order or warning when we had gone ten yards.

Or even:

> The procession stopped short suddenly when we had gone ten yards without any order or warning.

By placing 'Suddenly' and 'when we had gone ten yards' at the beginning of the sentence, Orwell breaks the normal word order – and gains a significant emphatic effect. By placing them at the beginning of the sentence, he draws attention to these words, thus emphasising the suddenness, the quickness and the location of the event that caused the procession to stop.

The adverbs can be in the form of prepositional phrases, again at the beginning of sentences: look out for 'In the first place', 'After that', 'Originally', 'Eventually' or such like at the beginning of sentences, drawing attention in this case to time, but it could be place or manner (e.g., 'Condescendingly, she allowed him to escort her to the prom ...').

Worked example

Note the following sentence taken from an education article:

> Many secondary schools in Scotland seem to be ignoring official guidance on the new curriculum, a poll has found.

The main clause 'a poll has found' has been placed at the end of the sentence, which is quite a common technique used by journalists. Here the most important piece of news is the fact that most secondary schools in Scotland seem to be ignoring new curriculum guidance – and not that a poll found this to be the case. Therefore, that piece of information comes first to engage the reader.

(d) long and short sentences

When there is a long sentence, or even a series of long sentences followed by a short one, then the effect is invariably dramatic, drawing attention to the short sentence.

Worked example

The following extract is from an Orwell essay – *Shooting an Elephant*. It has been reported to Orwell that an elephant has gone 'must' and, since in a mad fit it had killed someone, it has to be shot. Here he describes the shooting of the elephant.

> I fired a third time. That was the shot that did for him. You could see the agony of it jolt his whole body and knock the last remnant of strength from his legs. But in falling he seemed for a moment to rise, for as his hind legs collapsed beneath him he seemed to tower upwards like a huge rock toppling, his trunk reaching skywards like a tree. He trumpeted, for the first and only time. And then down he came, his belly towards me, with a crash that seemed to shake the ground even where I lay.
>
> I got up. The Burmans were already racing past me across the mud.

(continued)

Here you can actually feel the dramatic effect of the short sentence at the beginning of the second paragraph following the long sentence at the end of the previous one. Let's examine more closely what makes this particular device so dramatic:

- The short sentence is only three monosyllabic words long – thereby understating the action, leaving the emotions felt by the writer to the reader's imagination. The reader can therefore sympathise with the writer's feelings as he gets up after killing the elephant – something he did not want to do.

- The contrast between the long sentence and the short one is highlighted by its very shortness – but also the two sentences highlight the drama of the slowness and noise of the elephant's fall in contrast with the simplicity and ease of the writer's upward movement: 'I got up'.

- Note also the link between the two sentences – the last one of the first paragraph ends with the shaking of the ground where the author lay, while the short sentence uses the words 'I got up': the use of 'where I lay' and 'I got up' forms an excellent link between the two paragraphs, linking the drama of the death of the elephant with the simple action of getting up.

(e) unusual word groups

Occasionally, an author uses an unusual expression or combination of words in order to draw attention to the point being made.

Worked example

Look at the following quotation from *The Embankment* by the poet T. E. Hulme:

> Oh, God, make small
> The old star-eaten blanket of the sky,
> That I may fold it round me and in comfort lie.

The line 'The old star-eaten blanket of the sky' is a highly unusual expression, which recalls the term 'old moth-eaten blanket'. Just as an old moth-eaten blanket is one which has been around for so long that moths have left many small holes in it, so the stars look like holes in the blanket of the sky. The metaphor is developed when the persona talks about folding the blanket round him as he lies (presumably) out in the open. Such unusual expressions are often powerful metaphors, breathing new life into outworn expressions. They are the very opposite of clichés.

A binary expression, on the other hand, is when a writer links two words or expressions to gain rhythm and often drama; they can have the effect of arresting the reader's attention.

Worked example

Read the following extract from Jonathan Miller's *The Body in Question*:

For such reasons blood has always been regarded as a form of natural wealth: a rich liquid asset settled on each individual as a birthright, a priceless deposit which can neither be spent nor accumulated, only lost or dispersed through injury or ill-health. There are no plutocrats, only paupers. Adequacy is abundance.

Note the use of binaries: *natural wealth: a rich liquid asset*; *can neither be spent nor accumulated*; *only lost or dispersed*; *injury or ill-health*; *no plutocrats, only paupers*; *Adequacy is abundance.*

Notice, though, the last binary: Adequacy is abundance. It's not a binary opposite as such, but there is almost a kind of oxymoron lurking there that is effective in that it makes the reader think again about meaning – if you have sufficient blood in your veins then you have an abundance in that you are richly healthy.

Important point

Oxymoron is the placing side by side of terms or ideas that are contradictory or suggest a contrast.

Important point

Some definitions of oxymoron state that it is the juxtaposition of contradictory terms, but watch the word 'juxtaposition': it means placing side by side and does NOT mean or even imply contrast.

(f) the use of questions/imperatives/punctuation marks/parenthesis

Questions

Sentences that form questions are called interrogatives; and sentences that form commands are termed 'imperatives'. That just leaves statements and interjections (Eh! Ah!) and we have labelled the four types of sentences:

Statement	–	I walk
Interrogative/question	–	Do I walk?
Imperative/command	–	Walk!
Interjection/exclamation	–	Eugh!

Note the importance of punctuation! Questions and imperatives are signalled by either a question mark (?) or an exclamation mark (!). Be alert to these punctuation marks when being asked about the contribution made by sentence structure to whatever task is identified in the question.

Worked example

The following example from the 2009 Higher paper should make things clear. The writer, Leo Hickman, had attended a conference in Switzerland entitled 'Aviation and Environment Summit': it was planned to assess how damaging flying is to the environment. In this extract, he records what some of the speakers said:

> Speaker after speaker bemoaned how the public had somehow misunderstood the aviation industry and had come to believe that aviation is a huge and disproportionate polluter. Let's get this into perspective, said repeated speakers: this is small fry compared with cars, factories, even homes. Why are we being singled out, they cried? Why not, they said, chase after other industries that could easily make efficiency savings instead of picking on an industry that gives so much to the world, yet is currently so economically fragile?
>
> Adapted from *The Guardian*, 20 May 2006

Q Show how the writer's use of language conveys his unsympathetic view of the speakers at the conference. Refer to at least **two** features such as sentence structure, tone, word choice ...

The aposiopesis at the end of the list of language features indicates that candidates need not be restricted to those three features.

Let's deal with sentence structure. And, of course, you will have already spotted the two question marks – so what can we say about how these two questions convey his unsympathetic view of the speakers? Often in a situation where someone (such as, in this case, speakers for the aviation industry) is pleading a fairly unpopular case, questions will be used to redirect, and thereby distract, the listener's (or reader's) attention to other aspects of the subject in hand, mainly to avert blame from him or herself.

> **Important point !**
>
> Note carefully! Aposiopesis refers to the three dots at the end of a sentence, suggesting an unfinished thought, whereas ellipsis refers to the three dots in the middle of a sentence or paragraph, suggesting that words have been omitted.

Such questions are intended to be rhetorical, implying their own answers – in this case, the first question implies that the aviation industry believes it ought not to get the sole blame because there are others as blameworthy. The second question implies that it would be better to pick on other less 'economically fragile' industries, especially when aviation is so altruistic, performing such a service to the entire world. Clearly, Hickman thinks that by posing these rhetorical questions the speakers are performing a diversionary tactic so that aviation can (wrongly) escape blame, thereby showing his disapproval.

You can also argue that by repeating these questions, especially with the inserted 'they cried' and 'they said', asked at the conference by speakers, Hickman conveys a mocking tone. But more than that: the fact that he does use 'they cried' and 'they said' suggests that the questions are in the form of reported or direct speech, yet the lack of inverted commas indicates that these words weren't spoken by any one individual – they represent the kind of complaints frequently made by a number of speakers – whingeing, peevish, annoying complaints associated with those who see the industry as innocent victims vilified by an unfair campaign. All these

(continued)

make clear his disapproval by his mordant use of scorn. (If you are unfamiliar with its meaning, look up 'mordant'.) The lack of punctuation marks (in this case the lack of inverted commas) is, of course, a feature of punctuation.

But the observant reader will also have noticed other uses of punctuation in the above paragraph: the colon.

Let's get this into perspective, said repeated speakers: this is small fry compared with cars, factories, even homes.

The colon has three main uses: (a) to signal the introduction of a list; (b) to signal an explanation after a statement; (c) to introduce a quotation.

In this case, the colon is signalling the substance (i.e. an explanation) of what each speaker said – that there are other, greater causes of pollution than the aviation industry.

Punctuation (including parenthesis)

There are other punctuation marks with which you should be familiar:

Important point

Remember that punctuation is always used to clarify meaning for, or signal meaning to, the reader.

Punctuation mark	Example	Explanation of usage
Comma ,	This number is being played live, in response to many requests, by Simple Minds.	Used to clarify the text and avoid ambiguity. The commas are needed to clarify that it wasn't Simple Minds who were making the request! Also used in simple lists to separate straightforward items. In a sentence with two main clauses, a comma is needed if there is a second subject but not needed if the second verb shares the subject. A comma is also needed after an adjunct that has been placed at the beginning of a sentence.
Semi-colon ;	I have a girlfriend; her name is Mandy 'We recognised them instantly: the foreign place names such as the Somme and Ypres; the lines of men at the recruiting office; the rows of crosses in war cemeteries; the scarlet poppies blowing in the fields.'	In a sentence, the semi-colon can be used to indicate an interconnection between items which in themselves could stand as grammatically independent sentences. To separate items in a complex list where commas would be insufficient or where commas are already used in items within the list.
Colon :	'The isle is the most desolate place I have ever seen: its docks deserted, windows smashed, walls spray-gunned.'	To introduce a list. To signal an explanation following a statement. To introduce a quotation.
Paired dash and paired brackets Paired comma – (Parenthesis) – , parenthesis,	I often go to the cinema – the one off Union Street – on Friday evenings Or I met Kevin at the cinema last night – he often goes there on Fridays – and he told me about the strangest happening.	To isolate information which is additional to the sentence but grammatically separate from it. What is in parenthesis is syntactically independent.

(continued)

Punctuation mark	Example	Explanation of usage
Paired comma , interpolation,	This occurs when a phrase has been inserted into the sentence but, unlike parenthesis, the phrase is part of the grammar. The phrase 'unlike parenthesis' in the previous sentence is an example of interpolation.	Often used in climax to delay the main point to the end of the sentence.
Paired comma , apposition,	When a phrase is used to explain a term, while performing the same grammatical function as the word or phrase that it explains. For example, Nicola Sturgeon, Scotland's First Minister, said in the Chamber yesterday … The phrase *Scotland's First Minister* is in apposition to Nicola Sturgeon – it explains who she is – and both are part of the subject of the verb *said*. It is acceptable to regard both interpolation and apposition as a form of parenthesis.	In formal English, the phrase in apposition – i.e. the explanatory phrase – comes after the main term as in the example opposite, but in informal English – such as the tabloid press – the explanatory phrase often comes first. For example: Scotland's First minister, Nicola Sturgeon, said in the Chamber yesterday … You are not likely to be asked about phrases in apposition, but knowledge of them can be useful in identifying the formality of a text.
Single dash –	You know I have always regarded maths as difficult – less so as I get older.	To indicate an afterthought or, more recently, to replace the colon after a statement and before the explanation.

Punctuation mark	Example	Explanation of usage
Inverted commas "inverted commas" OR 'inverted commas'	Inverted commas are used to signal titles of works – "Macbeth". Their use makes clear that you are discussing the play and not the character. Also used to indicate that a word is being used in an unusual way or used to mean something different from its usual meaning: it's nasty if you are 'thumped' on the head by an asteroid. Also used to indicate direct speech or quotation, though most frequently used to indicate irony. Sometimes, *italics* are used in place of inverted commas.	To indicate the words actually used by a speaker in direct speech; the words of a quotation; titles of books, plays, films, etc.; or to indicate a word used in an unusual way or slightly out of context; to suggest a word is being used ironically.
Apostrophe	don't can't John's book	To denote the contraction of a word by the omission of a letter or letters. To indicate possession.
Aposiopesis	The three dots at the end of a sentence …	A device to indicate the sudden ending of speech or line of thought, indicating a trailing off, a change in subject, or an unwillingness to continue … To suggest that something is being left to the reader's imagination.
Ellipsis	The three dots in the middle of a sentence.	A device to indicate that some words have been missed out: *To be, or not to be* *That is the question* *Whether 'tis … end them*

You may not be asked directly about any given punctuation mark, but bear in mind that, since punctuation is used to signal meaning to the reader, you can sometimes use the punctuation mark to decode meaning. For example, although you may not be asked about the function of a colon, you may be asked to put an explanation of a piece of text into your own words, the relevant explanation of which may well be signalled by a colon.

Worked example

An example will make this clearer. Read carefully the following paragraph taken from a *Scotsman* article by George Kerevan:

> There is a stock response to my love affair with libraries: that I am being too nostalgic. That the multi-tasking, MTV generation can access information from a computer, get cheap books from the supermarket and still chatter to each other at a thousand decibels.
>
> Who needs old-fashioned library buildings? And why should councils subsidise what Google can provide for free?

Q Explain, according to the writer, what the stock response is to his love affair with libraries.

It would seem, at first glance, that there are several stock responses, all set out in the above paragraph. But look carefully at the first line where the colon is signalling the answer – that he is being too nostalgic, that he is yearning wistfully for an era that has passed. The rest of the paragraph is a kind of development of that notion: no matter how much he longs for libraries, the younger generation has plenty of alternatives that don't depend on contributions from local authorities.

And, of course, you have noticed the questions? It appears that these are the questions that those who concur with the MTV generation would ask. But do you also detect tone? The writer, by his use of these questions, is being sarcastic, even scornful, about the MTV generation's preference for the superficial, dismissive world of laptop trivia.

(g) a sudden switch in tense

Writers sometimes switch tense – from the past to the present or from the future to the present – usually to affirm immediacy.

Worked example

Look at the following paragraph adapted from a tabloid newspaper:

Spaceguard director, Jay Tate, explains: 'In the longer term the problem of being hit by an asteroid will be the amount of material that is injected into the Earth's atmosphere. Within two or three days the surface of the Earth will be cold and dark. And it is the dark which will be the problem, because the plants will begin to die out. At best guess, we will probably lose about 25 per cent of the human population of the planet in the first six months or so. The rest of us are basically back in the Middle Ages. We have got no power, no communications, no infrastructure. We are back to hunter-gathering.'

Q Show how the language used by Jay Tate emphasises the catastrophic effects of an asteroid smashing into the Earth. (4 marks)

You must remember that questions about language mean that you should consider word choice, sentence structure, tense, imagery, punctuation, tone. For a 4-mark question, it's an idea to have two examples of word choice and a developed answer involving sentence structure, though often it's safer to provide four different examples.

(continued)

In this case, let's look at the switch in tense. But first of all, we need to be clear about what we mean by the tense of a language. The infinitive of a verb is the part with the word 'to' in front: e.g. to swim, to run, to be, to have, to write, to read ...

Each verb has several tenses – most importantly, present, past and future. Let's take the verb 'to jump':

Present tense	I jump (or I am jumping, I do jump)
Past tense	I jumped (or I was jumping, I have jumped, I did jump)
Future tense	I shall jump, they will jump

Now look again at the paragraph above. Note that to begin with Tate uses the future tense: he uses 'will be' and 'will begin' and 'will probably lose', but then he changes to the present tense in the final three sentences:

> The rest of us *are* basically back in the Middle Ages. We *have got* no power, no communications, no infrastructure. We *are* back to hunter-gathering.

The writer is using the tense to reflect the immediacy of the impact, reinforcing its suddenness, making it clear that there is no time to escape its horror. Here the present tense stresses the present-ness, the here-and-now of the situation, which in turn creates immediacy, drawing attention to what is happening now.

(h) repetition

Often, as part of sentence structure, a writer will use repetition, otherwise known as anaphora. Be aware of its use and think about the ways in which the repetition contributes to the rhythm of the particular sentence and therefore to the meaning.

Worked example

In this sentence from an article in *The Sunday Herald* by Rebecca McQuillan, note the repetition of 'usually':

> We have all heard of the 'crazy cat lady', the woman, usually older, usually single, whose numerous cats get the run of the house.

In the above sentence the repetition of 'usually' gives the parenthetical 'usually older, usually single' a particular rhythm which helps to draw attention to the meaning – the description of the cat women.

Rhythm can, of course, contribute to other kinds of sentence structure, such as climax.

Tone or mood

To deal appropriately with questions about tone, you often have to examine sentence structure and word choice. An example will make this clear. In the following extract, a parent, in a letter to a national newspaper, makes comments on the proposal to save money by closing schools to pupils on Friday afternoons.

Worked example

Read the extract carefully and then answer the question that follows:

> It is quite intolerable for the council to even think about closing schools on Friday afternoons. It is simply increasing the costs to parents in increased childcare fees, and that is unfair and unjust. In any case, children get plenty of holidays – two weeks at Christmas, two weeks in October, a long weekend in February, two weeks at Easter, seven long weeks in the summer – so the last thing they need is time off. For families who work this is going to cause unfair disruption if not downright hardship.

(continued)

Q By referring to an example, analyse how the writer's use of language conveys her tone of disapproval about the council's proposal. (2 marks)

Important point

Remember that the term 'language' covers sentence structure, word choice, imagery, punctuation and tone.

Tone often can be inferred (deduced) by the examination of sentence structure and word choice. In this case, it can be answered by word choice: words and phrases such as 'intolerable', 'even to think about', 'iniquitous', 'disruption', 'somewhat craftily' and 'downright hardship' all have the connotation of disapproval. Each of those words and phrases not only suggest her disapproval, but also her annoyance at the council's proposals.

So far, we have just made a comment. Now we have to demonstrate by analysis how the terms actually suggest disapproval and annoyance. Let's take one of them: the writer refers to the council as moving 'somewhat craftily' to increase parental costs. You have to say in what way 'craftily' suggests disapproval. Look to the connotations of the word: 'craftily' suggests someone acting in a sly, cunning, devious way. The word is pejorative. Therefore our answer has to make clear that by the writer's use of 'somewhat craftily', she is suggesting that the council is being devious and underhand, thereby expressing her disapproval of the council's actions. Moreover, by the use of the adjective 'somewhat' she is deliberately using meiosis, deliberately understating her criticism, in order to draw attention to and highlight the slyness of the council's action.

But to what extent does the writer's use of sentence structure convey this tone of concern? Look at the second sentence: 'By adopting this move to save money, the council, somewhat craftily, is simply increasing the costs to parents in increased childcare fees, and that is unfair and unjust.' You can't help but notice the use of climax, ending in the words 'unfair' and 'unjust', thus highlighting the writer's disapproval. The climax is strengthened in this long sentence by piling up phrases – 'By adopting this move to save money' and 'somewhat craftily' – thus delaying the main point to the end.

The climax – 'and that is unfair and unjust' – is also further highlighted and made conspicuous by being isolated by the use of the comma and the 'and', which has the effect of separating it, isolating it, from the rest of the sentence, thereby drawing attention to it.

But consider also the contribution made by the **parenthesis** to the tone of disapproval. Parenthesis is information separated from and additional to the rest of the sentence by paired dashes, brackets or commas. The information, by having been separated, is thus highlighted. In this case, the use of parenthesis isolates and draws attention to the information about the amount of holidays pupils have ' – two weeks at Christmas, two weeks in October, a long weekend in February, two weeks at Easter, seven long weeks in the summer – '. Because the writer lists the sheer amount of holidays pupils have, she is registering her disapproval by suggesting that they are plentiful and that therefore no more are needed, while the word 'long' in the phrase 'seven long weeks in the summer', reinforces and intensifies her tone of disapproval by suggesting that these holidays are over-lengthy.

The link sentence

It is really important that any piece of prose is cohesively written – in other words, ideas have to 'flow' from one paragraph to the next by using linkage.

Worked example

For example, the following extract, by the columnist Ian Bell, is from an article about the minimum pricing of alcohol. Here, he is considering the confusion caused by the addition of the phrase 'Drink responsibly' to alcohol products and advertising:

(continued)

> Like any industry, the alcohol business wants to shift as much product as it can manufacture. The bosses of drinks firms don't get together periodically to decide that a billion gallons is enough to be going on with. If we're swallowing, they're selling.
>
> Given that fact, it is hardly surprising that five European countries would object to the Scottish Government's plan for minimum pricing. Each of the five – France, Spain, Italy, Portugal and Bulgaria – produces oceans of wine and lakes of spirits. They are all for responsible drinking, but not if it affects profits, and certainly not if it is backed by legislation.
>
> *Sunday Herald*, 28 July 2013

There is an actual formula for answering this kind of question: (a) quote the phrase that links back – look for words such as 'all this' or 'that' or 'these' or 'therein' or 'therefore', etcetera.; (b) demonstrate the link back to the idea contained in the previous paragraph; (c) quote the words that link forward to the idea of the new paragraph; (d) demonstrate the link forward to that idea.

Let's apply the formula. Clearly, the phrase 'Given that fact' refers back to the idea in the previous paragraph that producers of alcohol will try to sell as much as they produce, while the expression 'five European countries would object to minimum pricing' leads, in the current paragraph, to the stated reason for their objections.

Worked example

The following extract is from Bill Bryson's biography, *Shakespeare*, in which he discusses, among other aspects of Shakespeare's life, the conditions endured by actors at that time. In this section, Bryson is demonstrating the demands made by the theatre companies, demands which meant that actors, even though they were each playing many parts, had to be in position, on cue, appropriately dressed, and equipped with the relevant props. Failure to do so led to enormous fines. Bryson goes on:

That in itself must have been a challenge, for nearly all clothing then involved either complicated fastenings – two dozen or more obstinate fabric clasps on a standard doublet – or yards of lacing.

In such a hothouse, reliability was paramount. Henslowe's papers [Henslowe was a theatrical entrepreneur in Shakespeare's time] show that actors were subjected to rigorous contractual obligations, with graduated penalties for missing rehearsals, being drunk or tardy, failing to be 'ready apparelled' at the right moment, or – strikingly – for wearing stage costumes outside the playhouse.

Q Demonstrate the ways in which the first sentence of the second paragraph acts as a link between the paragraphs.

Important point!

Remember the formula: quote, link back; quote, demonstrate link forward.

In this case, the word 'such' in the expression 'in such a hothouse' links back to the idea that changing costumes quickly enough was a challenge for Elizabethan actors (the word 'such' clearly refers to an antecedent – a word or object that has already been mentioned). Then the expression 'reliability was paramount' anticipates the subject of the paragraph, the ways in which actors had to be reliable.

The structure of the passage

Structure, invariably, has to do with linkage, therefore this type of question is usually a form of the link question. The question usually asks about the way in which a paragraph links the ideas between two sections of the passage. You tackle this task in a similar way to questions about link sentences: identify the words that link back to the ideas already discussed and demonstrate that link, then identify the words that link forward into the ideas about to be explored.

Summarising some of the arguments

One of the most important skills assessed in the RUAE paper is your ability to summarise aspects of a writer's argument.

Summarising involves presenting the gist of a writer's argument, the main points, the synopsis or précis of his or her line of thought. You should omit examples and any figures of speech.

Worked example

Read the following passage carefully – it is an extract from a previous past paper (2013 Passage A). The author, Carol Midgley, reflects on the appeal of shopping in our culture of consumption:

How did we get to a point where shopping became the premier leisure activity, where we gladly boarded the work-to-spend treadmill, the insatiable pursuit of 'more', which resulted in there being, for example, 121 mobile phones for every 100 people in the UK? Does it even matter? Shopping doesn't kill anyone, it keeps the economy going and provides one in six jobs. If it makes people happy, why not leave them to it?

Well, that's just it. Turbo-consumerism – the age of instant gratification and voracious appetite for 'stuff' – cannot make us happy and it never will. Every time we are seduced into buying one product, another appears that is 'new', 'improved', better than the one you have. Turbo-consumerism is the heroin of human happiness, reliant on the fact that our needs are never satisfied. A consumer society can't allow us to stop shopping and be content because then the whole system would die. Instead it has to sell us just enough to keep us going but never enough that our wants are satisfied. The brief high we feel is compensation for not having a richer, fuller life.

For years, shops, retail centres, giant malls have been taking over public spaces worldwide, creating a mainstream monoculture. The pedestrianisation of city centres, though largely regarded as pro-citizen, is in fact primarily to maximise 'footfall' and shoppers' 'grazing time'. This retail creep has ensured that increasingly there's not much else to do but shop. The more we consume, the less space there is to be anything other than consumers. The space to be citizens and make decisions equally and collectively about the world around us is diminished. It may be a free country, but we simply have the freedom to shop. Kings as consumers, pawns as citizens.

Am I over-catastrophising the consumer phenomenon? In the Liverpool One shopping 'experience', where I am sitting, a place teeming with shoppers despite the credit crunch, and punctuated by *Massive Reductions!* signs, people don't look particularly disempowered or depressed. Purposeful, I suppose, but also strangely distracted, as if they do not notice the environment around them, merely the magnetic shop signs. I understand the siren call of TK Maxx and how a £3 top can mend a bad day. But the question is, why does it?

There are nearly 400 words in that passage and we need to reduce it considerably in order to summarise it effectively. What is the argument? Bear in mind that it is the structure of the argument that is required. Ignore any extras such as any illustrations, anecdotes, examples, imagery. Let's enumerate the basic stages:

(a) How did shopping become the foremost leisure activity and why do we devote our time and money to its pursuit?

(b) If it is a harmless activity, does it matter that shopping is the be-all and end-all of existence?

(c) But shopping, she claims, cannot make people happy, simply because we can never be satisfied – new, improved products continually demand to be bought;

(d) The consumer society cannot allow us to stop shopping or else it will collapse – we have to be given only enough to ensure that our wants are never fully met;

(e) Retail is invading all aspects of our society and even pedestrianised city streets exist to maximise the number of shoppers;

(f) Increasingly there is nothing much else for people to do than shop.

(continued)

Those are the stages of the argument, but what is the real line of thought? There are three parts to her argument, which are based on the question – 'how did shopping become the premier leisure activity?' The three parts are: (a) since shopping doesn't injure anyone, since it stimulates economic growth and since it makes people happy, there can't be much harm, can there? (b) the answer to that question: it cannot make people happy because shopping can never satisfy – the whole retail process ensures that each product is replaced by a different design and the one just bought becomes instantly out-of-date; (c) town planning is geared to maximising consumer spend, leaving shopping as the supreme leisure and cultural pursuit, thus minimising freedom for other city-dwelling pursuits.

You can set out the answer in the (a), (b), (c) structure above or you can write it out as formal prose. A bullet-point layout is probably less time-consuming.

Inferences

To infer means to make deductions, to make clear your conclusions from your reading of a piece of text.

Worked example

Look again at the extract above from Carol Midgley's reflections on shopping. Read the third paragraph carefully, then think about the following question: from what the writer has said, what can you deduce about her views about the pedestrianisation of city centres?

To answer such questions about inference or deductions you really have to use the evidence in front of you. What does the writer actually say? She makes several points:

Point 1 – The pedestrianisation of city centres, though largely regarded as pro-citizen, is in fact primarily to maximise 'footfall' and shoppers' 'grazing time'.

Point 2 – This retail creep has ensured that increasingly there's not much else to do but shop. The more we consume, the less space there is to be anything other than consumers.

Point 3 – The space to be citizens and make decisions equally and collectively about the world around us is diminished. It may be a free country, but we simply have the freedom to shop. Kings as consumers, pawns as citizens.

We can deduce, then, that (1) Midgley believes that pedestrianisation is for the benefit of the retail outlets and not for the benefit of citizens; (2) she believes that such spread of pedestrianisation has reduced space for people to use in ways other than shopping, and the more we shop the more pedestrianisation spreads; and (3) we have less and less space to be free to consider aspects of the world around us, because we are forced to focus our thoughts on shopping.

To answer inference questions you have to be a bit like a crime-scene investigator: examine the evidence closely and see where it takes you!

The skill in being able to infer is, perhaps, even more useful when it comes to analysing aspects of literary texts.

3. Questions about evaluation

To answer questions that ask you to evaluate, you must make a judgement on the effect of the language and/or the ideas of the passage(s), such as questions about conclusions.

Conclusions

Questions about conclusions often involve evaluation. In answering such a question you should try to identify some obvious characteristics of a good conclusion. You need to read the question carefully and note:

(a) Does the question ask about the effectiveness of the conclusion, in which case you are free to say that it is effective, that it is not effective, or that it is partially effective, with reasons given in each case?

(b) Is the question about how the ideas are concluded?

(c) Is it about the effectiveness of language as a conclusion?

(d) Is it about both ideas and language?

In any case, look out for the following markers of an effective conclusion:

- a word (or idea) that signals summing up – 'Clearly', 'Thus';
- the use of the word 'And' at the beginning of a sentence or a paragraph – the word signals/draws attention to the fact that here is the final point and by isolating it in a sentence by itself, it highlights the summative effect of the sentence;
- an identifiable rhythm created by alliteration, lists, climax – how has the climax been delayed? Are there any phrases or words inserted to allow the main point to be kept dramatically to the end?
- any phrase or idea that is dramatic and/or memorable;
- an illustrative example of the ideas that have been discussed – an anecdote that has the effect of summing up or making an illustrative point made by the passage as a whole;
- the mention at the end of an image/idea/words already used at the beginning of the passage can have a rounding effect that is summative in nature;
- any references in the final paragraph that link back to ideas already dealt with.

4. Questions about both passages

In the RUAE exam, you will need to be able to make inferences and also to summarise the ideas of both passages.

There is only one question asked at the end of the second passage and since it is most likely to attract 5 marks, or 16% of the marks available, it is worth being clear about how to answer it.

Invariably you will be given a brief statement of the theme of both passages, after which you will be asked to identify key areas on which they agree – or disagree, as the case may be. The point is that the question will be about ideas, not about language or style.

First of all, you must identify the areas (of agreement/disagreement) – whatever the question demands.

- You must then refer in detail to both passages.
- You can use bullet points if you wish.
- Your evidence from both passages can be in the form of quotations, which MUST be supported by explanation.

For 5 marks – you must identify comprehensively three or more key areas with full use of supporting evidence.

For 4 marks – you must identify clearly three or more key areas with relevant use of supporting evidence.

For 3 marks – you have to identify three or more key areas with supporting evidence.

For 2 marks – you have to identify two areas with supporting evidence.

For 1 mark – you must identify one key area with supporting evidence.

Zero marks – you have failed to identify any key area and/or you have failed to understand the task.

A View from the Bridge

TWO ONE-ACT PLAYS BY

Arthur Miller

Author of DEATH OF A SALESMAN

a street car

named

desire

tennessee williams

The GREAT GATSBY

F·SCOTT·FITZGERALD

DEATH OF A SALESMAN

BY ARTHUR MILLER

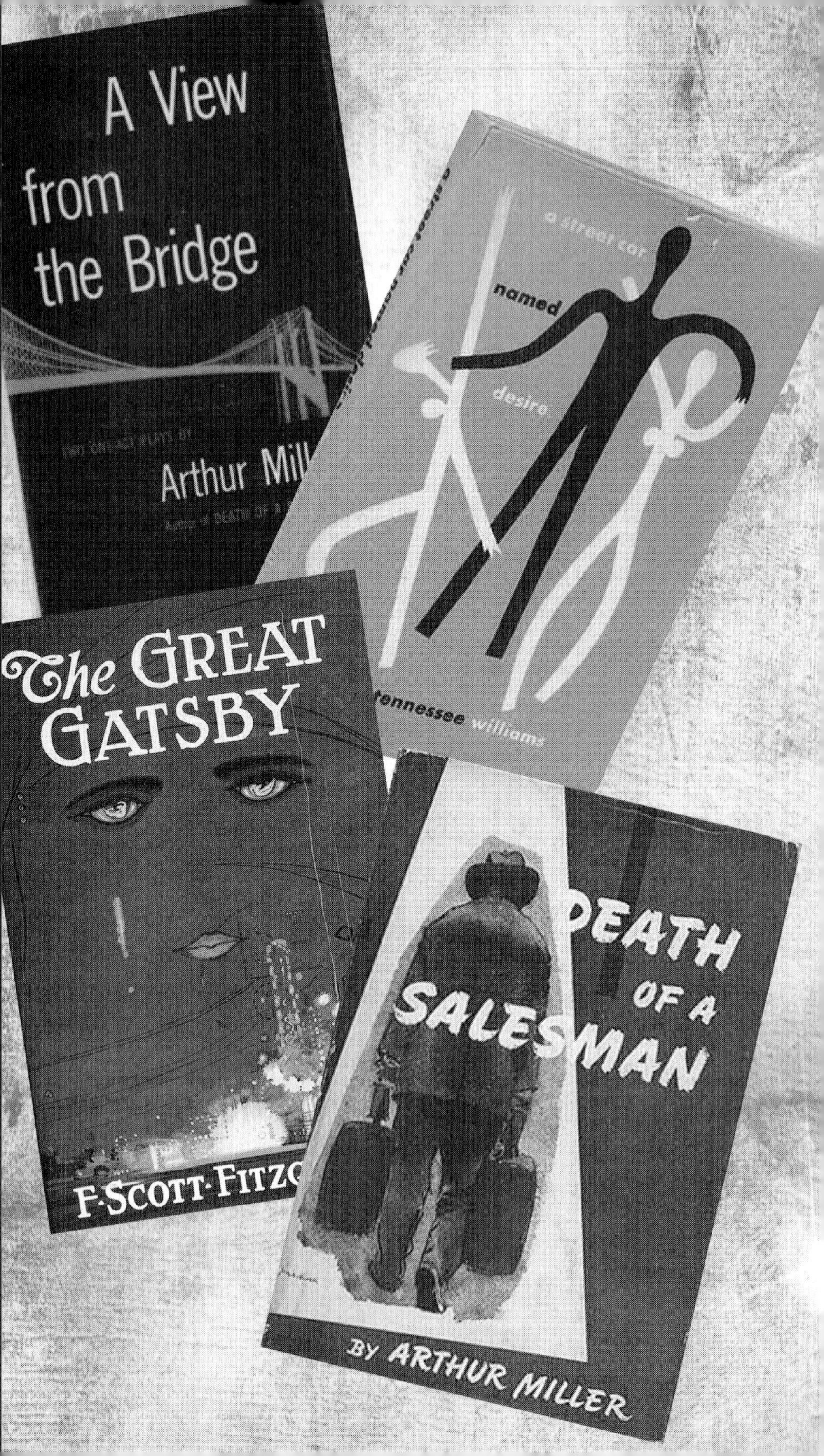

Critical Reading

There are two sections to the Critical Reading paper:

Section 1 – Scottish Text – 20 marks

Section 2 – Critical Essay – 20 marks

The Critical Reading paper, then, is worth 40% of the total marks available for Higher English, a significant amount.

By the end of this section you will know how best to approach the texts you are studying for the Critical Reading exam.

You need to know and understand, especially in drama and prose, the various aspects of the structure of texts: beginnings, endings, character presentation and development, conflict, setting in time and/or place, narrative technique, turning points, climax. You also need to know the theme(s) of the texts you are studying – themes such as family relationships, jealousy, sacrifice, societal values, violence, restoration of friendship, love, unrequited love, the moral and psychological growth of a young protagonist (main character), grief, alienation and so on.

How to approach drama and prose

Prose texts and drama texts may be set out differently on the page, but when it comes to analysis, there are sufficient similarities to enable us to deal with both together in this section of the book.

There are really only two questions you have to ask yourself when preparing your novel or play for the Critical Reading paper:

1. What is the text about? In other words, what is the theme?
2. What techniques has the novelist/playwright used to portray the theme?

Themes

It's worth spending some time thinking about what we mean by the word 'theme' and what constitutes a theme or themes. All stories, including folklore and fairy stories, make some kind of comment about people, about the world around us, about the society we live in; in other words, all literature makes comment about the human condition and human experience.

> **Important point**
>
> It is vitally important to recognise that theme is not a technique – the techniques are there to help portray theme(s).

Novels, short stories, plays, films, television drama serials all have something to say about love or jealousy or snobbery or pride or cruelty or rejection or even 'vaulting ambition'. We as readers or viewers usually recognise these 'themes' and often are able to re-examine our own experience in the light of them – that is, in the light of what we have read or seen on television, in the cinema or on stage.

But, as critics, we need also to examine *how* – the ways in which – the writer portrays or presents these themes. How does he or she manipulate setting or characterisation or symbolism to convey or explore the themes in such ways that we, the readers, the viewers, the audience can recognise them, relate to them and ultimately understand them? Therefore, as well as being able to recognise the theme of a novel or play, we also have to be able to recognise the techniques by which the writer has communicated the story and the theme to us.

> **Important point**
>
> You have to know about techniques such as narrative structure, characterisation, setting (time and/or place), symbolism, exposition, language, uses of conflict, turning point, climax, resolution and dénouement, some or all of which are used by writers to portray themes. In any case, critical essay questions often focus on such techniques.

There are, however, further aspects of prose fiction (and drama) that we have to consider before proceeding further.

The role of the author/narrator and meaning

Some people think that the work of fiction or drama is a means by which an author communicates with the reader, that the author has a message to convey, and that we, as readers, 'decode' that message, making remarks such as: 'Clearly, in *The Great Gatsby*, Fitzgerald is criticising the moral vacuum and snobbery of 1920s America'.

How *can* we know what authors mean? Do we text them and ask them? Invite them to come round and have a chat? (Not so easy when it comes to Shakespeare ...)

What matters above all is the **text**, not the author. Meaning has much less to do with the author's intention than the reader's own *interpretation* and *understanding* of the text. Meaning is the relationship that *you* have with the text. The reading process involves you – the reader – bringing your experiences and sensitivities, as well as your developed reading skills, to the text so that you can 'decode' the experiences, in your own terms.

But how does a story get told and who tells it? The author or the narrator?

The role of the narrator

Let's make a distinction between the author and the narrator of a story. It isn't an author who tells the story, it's a narrator – the author creates a narrator or a narrative voice. Of course, from time to time, an author can intrude and interrupt the narrator to make a point. Or sometimes the author just takes over for a bit. Henry James often intrudes to make a comment, and Jane Austen frequently makes heard her authorial voice.

But let's concentrate on the narrator – the voice that tells us the story.

There are various ways in which a novel can be narrated, the most important of which are set out below:

> **Important point**
>
> Remember that the term 'point of view' means the same as narrative technique – the way in which a story is told.

> **Important point**
>
> Although point of view is really an aspect of fiction, nevertheless a play can also have a narrator – for example, Alfieri in *A View from the Bridge* by Arthur Miller or Tom in *The Glass Menagerie* by Tennessee Williams.

1. ***Omniscient narrator*** – the story is told by a narrator (who has been created by the author); the author puts the narrator in the position of knowing everything about all the various settings and all the characters – about what

characters say, hear, see, feel, taste, smell. But more than that: he knows their most intimate thoughts and motivations better than they do themselves simply because the omniscient narrator knows everything.

2. **First person narration** – the story is told by one of the characters. The advantage of this method of narration is that the reader gets to know the character intimately and probably grows to like him/her, but the disadvantage is that the character telling the story has to be present at all times, otherwise he or she has to rely on others for information about episodes that took place before the novel began or about scenes at which he or she wasn't present. The reader's information is filtered through the mind of the character narrating the story, which means that there could be bias of which the reader is unaware.

The result of all this, of course, is that we cannot know the intimate thoughts of the other characters because the narrator (being a character in the novel and not omniscient) cannot know them him/herself. The character's narration can of course be prejudiced and therefore unreliable. In *The Great Gatsby* by Scott Fitzgerald, Nick Carraway is clearly prejudiced in favour of Gatsby, rendering his narrative fairly unreliable at times.

Sometimes there is multiple narration, where more than one character tells the story: the classic example of multiple narration is *Dracula* by Bram Stoker, where there are several narrators – Jonathan Harker, Dr Seward, Van Helsing, Mina Harker and Lucy Westenra, each of whom uses a different method of narrating the story. *Wuthering Heights* by Emily Brontë has two narrators – Lockwood and Nellie Dean.

3. **Third person narration** – the story is told by a third person narrator except that this time the narrator focuses only on one character and all events are seen through that character's eyes. The story is told in the third person but, since the narrator focuses on a particular character, that character is present at all times or has to rely on others. Many short stories are told in third person narration, where the **focus** is restricted to one character.

4. **Framed narrative** – the story is told within a story. For example, where a character narrates the story to another character who then narrates the story to the reader, or where a character in the story refers to another character who then tells the story. One of the most famous examples of a framed narrative is *Heart of Darkness* by Joseph Conrad, where one of the men on the boat waiting for the tide to turn on the Thames retells a story told to him by Marlow about his expedition to the Congo. He actually quotes Marlow, but occasionally interrupts Marlow's story to make comments of his own. It is 'framed' in that the author creates the first narrator who then makes use of a second narrator to tell the story to the reader.

Yet another good example of framed narrative is Henry James' intriguingly ambiguous tale *The Turn of the Screw*, in which there are in effect three narrators – an unnamed narrator and his friend, who is reading a manuscript written by a governess, now dead, but previously known to the friend. The story itself, then, is in effect told by the governess.

5. **Free indirect discourse** – the narrative is in the third person but written in such a way that the reader has access to the thinking of the characters in the story. This type of narration, developed by Jane Austen, is fairly common, and there are many examples of it in *The Cone Gatherers* by Robin Jenkins. An example from that novel will make this narrative technique clear.

The following extract comes from towards the very end of Chapter 1. Duror has followed the two cone gatherers back to their hut, which he then describes in some detail as:

> a greasy shed, hardly bigger than a rabbit-hutch, [that] had been knocked together in a couple of hours ... round about it was filthy with their refuse and ordure.

Such thoughts are not the thoughts of an objective, omniscient narrator; such thoughts are Duror's. We know that because of the comments: the word 'greasy' and the phrase 'knocked together in a couple of hours' are disparaging, fault-finding comments – clearly indicative of what Duror is thinking. Similarly, the words 'filthy with their refuse' express Duror's judgemental opinion. These are his thoughts, his criticisms of the two men whom he detests so much.

6. **Interior monologue** – the narrative is presented as the thoughts of one of the characters as they are going through his or her head. The narration is in the first person, but what often happens is that the narration switches from third person to first in order to make clear the character's thoughts as they go through his or her head. For example, in *Under the Skin* by Michel Faber, the novel begins in the third person, focusing on the main character, Isserley, but then it switches to interior monologue as we are presented with the thoughts of one of the hitch-hikers whom she picks up. Here is an example from Chapter 1 of the novel. This is the hitch-hiker thinking:

> She *drove* like a little old lady. Fifty miles an hour, absolute max. And that shoddy old anorak of hers on the back seat – what was that all about? She had a screw loose, probably. Nutter, probably. And she talked funny – foreign, definitely.

You can tell right away from the sentence structure – short sentences and minor sentences (sentences without a finite verb, such as 'Nutter, probably.') that these are the character's thoughts, exactly as he thinks them.

The difference between free indirect discourse and interior monologue is that the former retains the third person narration with access to the character's thoughts, whereas interior monologue involves the use of the first person to reveal the character's thoughts as they form in his/her mind.

Be sure you check the novel you are preparing for the exam to see which of the above techniques applies to the way the story is being told.

The role of time

Let's now examine the role of time in fiction and drama more closely. There are four ways in which the use of time is important in the structure of a novel or a play:

(i) The time in which the novel is set. In *Wuthering Heights* by Emily Brontë, for example, the very first word of the first chapter is '1801' – a very precise indication of the setting in time, with all the connotations and implications of a new millennium.

Sometimes we are not told the exact setting in time, but we can usually work it out from the level of technology present – if there are stagecoaches pulled by horses, the chances are the setting is pre-twentieth century.

(ii) The time when the work was written, sometimes referred to as the context, is an important aspect of the critical analysis of fiction and drama. No literary text is written in a vacuum; it is embedded in the historical, cultural, literary, societal, political context of its time. For example, *Of Mice and Men* by John Steinbeck is very much part of the era of the American Great Depression, which lasted from 1929 almost to the Second World War. Set in the 1930s, *Of Mice and Men* deals with the plight of landless migrant workers whose lives were the antithesis of the American Dream. That *All My Sons* by Arthur Miller was written just after the Second World War heightens the significance of Joe Keller's actions during the war in supplying faulty aircraft parts to the armed forces.

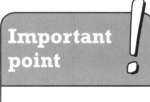

Important point

Find out about the relevant contexts of the text that you are reading at present.

(iii) The timescale over which the story is told. Sometimes the narrator tells us when the story begins, but often we have to work this out by paying attention to clues given by the narrator. In *The Great Gatsby* for example,

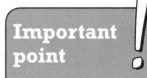

Important point

Short stories are often set over a very short period of time.

Nick Carraway, the narrator, is narrating the story in 1923 – 'when [he] came back from the East last autumn' – the year after which all the events had taken place. The technique is obviously flashback: the events that he recalls in 1923 are the events that took place in 1922.

The Great Gatsby begins in the early summer of 1922 and is set over a relatively short period of time – months rather than years. Short timescales tend to create an intensity, allow for a close examination of theme, whereas novels spread over long periods of time tend to allow for patterns to be detected and for several themes to be explored.

(iv) The time when the novel is read. It is important to bear in mind that there is inevitably a gap in time between when the work was written and the beginning of the twenty-first century when you are reading it. We should bear in mind that we as readers are possessed of the knowledge of all that has happened during that gap and that therefore we should be aware of how that knowledge might influence our reading of the text.

The role of structure

You now realise that one of the most important technical aspects of a text is its structure – the way in which the story has been put together by the author. All texts, poetry as well as novels, short stories, plays, essays, pieces of journalism, television dramas and films have been carefully structured by the writer (or director), and our job as critics is to unpick or deconstruct the ways in which the text has been built up.

But what do we mean by structure? As you already know from your general knowledge, the word 'structure' usually refers to the physical dimensions of objects or buildings – length, height, width – and each of these dimensions can be measured. The structure of, say, the Forth Bridge, however complex, can nevertheless be measured. When it comes to the written texts, though, these physical dimensions do not apply. What does apply, however, is the so-called 'fourth dimension' – time.

> ## Important point !
>
> *Analepsis* is a term used to refer to a scene at an earlier point in the story, while *prolepsis* is a term used to refer to a moment later in the chronological sequence of the story. A *proleptic scene*, for example, can be a moment of foreshadowing.

Linear structure

The structure of a novel or a play, then, has to do with the way in which the author deploys the use of time. After all, when you tell a story to your parents about what happened in school, you automatically structure your story in time: you give it a beginning, a middle and an ending. It's exactly the same with a novel or play – there is a beginning stage, a middle stage and an end stage; and many novels, more or less, follow this same pattern: a straightforward linear development.

Some stories, however, reverse the beginning and middle stages to form flashback, where the narrative begins in the middle of the story and then goes back to a beginning further back in time.

Important point

The term 'flashback' means a reversal of the beginning and middle stages of a text or where a text is written after the events, looking back at them – as in *The Great Gatsby* by Scott Fitzgerald or in *Jane Eyre* by Charlotte Brontë. On the other hand, the term 'analepsis' refers to a scene in which there are just references to former events.

Other stories, from time to time throughout the narrative, have scenes in which reference is made to points back in time, before the beginning, to give a character or the reader information about what happened before the story began – that kind of return to the past is not so much a flashback as an analeptic scene – more of which later.

Episodic structure

Another structural technique is where the text is in episodes, that is, scenes that appear to be almost contemporaneous, but which are related or linked thematically. Orwell's essay *Marrakech* is the perfect example of episodic structure. But, of course, although the episodes can take place at the same time or, indeed, at different times, nevertheless each episode in itself is linear, that is, structured in time. Film and some modern novels sometimes use such episodic structure.

You will find as you study the graphic below that the various stages in the structure of a novel or a play are often used as the basis for some critical

Important point

Remember that techniques are there to contribute to and portray theme. Many critical reading questions ask you to demonstrate the ways in which techniques do just that, though they may use different wording for theme, such as 'concerns of the text' or 'your understanding of the play/novel as a whole'.

essay questions. For example, there are often questions about beginnings, turning points, conflict, climaxes and endings. Such questions apply to drama as much as prose fiction.

Let's set out in graphic form the various stages in the timescale of a text:

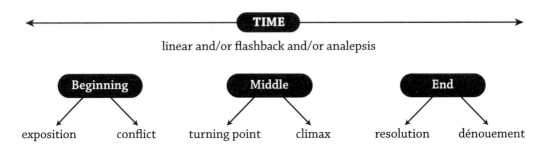

The six aspects structure – drama and novels

1. We have the ***exposition*** of the story – where the reader is given information about everything he or she needs to know to understand the story, including setting, characterisation, symbolism and who is to tell the story – the narrative technique;

2. then we have the ***development of conflict*** – stories, especially dramatic stories, cannot exist without conflict;

3. next is the ***turning point***, where the narrative changes direction, where the fortunes or fate of the main character alter and where we get a glimpse of the probable outcome of the narrative; the turning point is sometimes referred to by the term 'peripetaeia';

4. thereafter, there is the ***climax***, a technical term meaning the final point in the narrative where the protagonist (the main character) undergoes the very worst that can happen to him/her;

5. there then follows the ***resolution*** of the conflict and, ultimately, of the theme;

6. the final stage is referred to as the ***dénouement***, which draws together all the issues/themes and usually involves the ideas of restorative justice and redemption. 'Normal' social and moral order is restored.

The exposition

The very beginning of the novel or a play is often referred to as the exposition, where, in a novel, the point of view is made clear and we are introduced to the setting, the characters, symbolism and, of course, the plot.

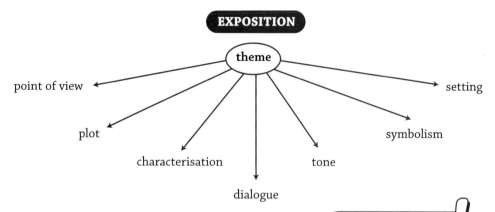

Remember the exposition isn't just the first few pages of the novel, but can sometimes stretch to a few chapters, until all these various aspects have been introduced. You should analyse each of these aspects for the ways in which theme is being established.

Important point

If you are asked a question about the beginning of a text, it's the exposition that you should be considering for your answer.

Worked example

Let's apply this theory to an actual example. We'll begin by examining the exposition of a drama text: *A Streetcar Named Desire* by Tennessee Williams. Here are the opening stage instructions. Read carefully the following extract:

SCENE ONE

The exterior of a two-storey corner building on a street in New Orleans which is named Elysian Fields and runs between the L & N tracks and the river. The section

(continued)

is poor but unlike corresponding sections in other American cities, it has a raffish charm. The houses are mostly white frame, weathered grey, with rickety outside stairs and galleries and quaintly ornamented gables. This building contains two flats, upstairs and down. Faded white stairs ascend to the entrances of both. It is first dark of an evening early in May. The sky that shows around the dim white building is a peculiarly tender blue, almost turquoise, which invests the scene with a kind of lyricism and gracefully attenuates the atmosphere of decay. You can almost feel the warm breath of the brown river beyond the river warehouses with their faint redolences of bananas and coffee. A corresponding air is evoked by the music of Negro entertainers at a bar-room around the corner. In this part of New Orleans you are practically always just around the corner, or a few doors down the street, from a tinny piano being played with the infatuated fluency of brown fingers. This 'blue piano' expresses the spirit of the life which goes on here.

[Two women, one white and one coloured, are taking the air on the steps of the building. The white woman is EUNICE, who occupies the upstairs flat; the coloured woman a neighbour, for New Orleans is a cosmopolitan city where there is a relatively warm and easy intermingling of races in the old part of town.

Above the music of the 'blue piano' the voices of people on the street can be heard overlapping.]

The sheer length of these stage instructions strongly suggests that Williams intended them to be read. How, for example, does a director indicate on stage that Elysian Fields 'runs between the L & N tracks and the river'? Such information is clearly intended for a reader. It is important that you study and are able to refer to the stage instructions of the play you are studying.

Since these instructions (above) are part of the exposition, we need to look for the ways in which Williams has established setting, characterisation, symbolism, tone and plot. In this particular example, so far, we really only have setting. The reference to Elysian Fields is symbolic: it was, in Greek mythology, the final resting place for the

Important point !

Again, note the way in which the text has been analysed: first of all a point is made, illustrated by close textual reference, followed by relevant analytical comment. This procedure is referred to as textual analysis, which forms some of the questions in Section 1 of the paper – the Scottish text section.

souls of the valiant and the righteous. Given that the name of the area is Elysian Fields and that this same area is 'poor', albeit with a 'raffish charm', we become aware of the ironic contrast between paradise and poverty. There is also foreshadowing implied in that Elysium is a place for the dead and Blanche has just walked into it, implying that the theme of death is a major theme in the play.

We are also told the setting in time: it is an evening in early May, when the 'tender blue' of the sky 'invests the scene with a kind of lyricism' that 'attenuates the atmosphere of decay'. Again we have contrast between beauty and decay, though the decay is softened somewhat by the beauty – the reference to 'a kind of lyricism' – and the use of the word 'attenuates' suggests that the decay has been reduced in force or strength.

Again, expressions such as 'You can almost feel the warm breath of the brown river … with their faint redolences of bananas and coffee' are fairly obviously intended for the benefit of the reader. The implication here is of warm, pleasing, exotic smells, the scents of faraway places.

Clearly, the director, the set designer, the lighting and sound engineers, the costume designer and the actors must communicate to an audience the complexity of this setting, along with the suggestions that we have noted. An important part of this setting is the 'music of Negro entertainers', which pervades the streets and contributes to the atmosphere of raffish charm and 'the spirit of life'. The sound of the blue piano is repeated in many of the scenes.

The appearance of the two women – 'one white and one coloured' – who are 'taking the air on the steps of the building', contributes not only to the mood of relaxation but also to the lack of racial tension. The short scene between them symbolises the cosmopolitan nature of New Orleans.

> **Important point**
>
> Check and record the meanings of 'raffish', 'attenuate', 'redolence', and 'allure' if you are uncertain.

> **Important point**
>
> Sometimes, a writer chooses to subvert the exposition, deliberately obscuring aspects of point of view, plot, characterisation, symbolism, tone and dialogue in order to confuse or bewilder readers by leading them in the wrong direction for dramatic effect. Does this apply to the text you are studying? Michel Faber's *Under the Skin* is an example of subverted exposition.

(continued)

The setting is symbolic, vibrant and colourful, appealing to all our senses, and suggesting life and magnetic allure, into which walks the delicate, fragile and vulnerable Blanche DuBois, all of which foreshadows her downfall. Williams' use of setting, contrast and symbolism help establish the themes of death and destruction.

Note the importance of lighting and sound, especially the choice of music. It's worth going through your drama text and noting what lighting and sounds are used and their effect on the themes.

The role of conflict

Novels and drama really have to involve conflict. Sometimes, in the more basic plots, the conflict is straightforward: good versus evil, illustrated by stories about cops-versus-robbers or MI5-versus-terrorists or David-versus-Goliath (e.g. a small, insignificant person versus a large, powerful corporation).

Sometimes, however, the conflict isn't derived from the opposition of 'goodies' or 'baddies' but stems from two sets of opposing attitudes or values: television serial dramas, such as *Coronation Street*, *Emmerdale*, *Eastenders*, *Hollyoaks*, tend to explore this conflict of opposing sets of attitudes or values between or within families.

More 'serious' novels and plays, however, invariably explore the conflict between the good and the morally deficient. In such texts, conflict is established between the main character or hero and what are called the 'antagonistic forces', usually set in motion by a catalyst, then developed as the narrative progresses. It takes time (usually) to build up the conflict, the author developing it in all kinds of ways, some explicit, some very subtle.

> **Important point**
>
> You can't have drama without conflict. Whichever play you are studying, make sure that you know *how* the conflict is established and *how* it is developed.

> **Important point**
>
> A catalyst is a scene or event or even the entrance of a character, the effect of which is to trigger or speed up the conflict within the story. For example, the scene with the ghost (Act I scenes 4 and 5) is the catalyst in *Hamlet*; the catalyst in Macbeth is the scene where the witches meet Macbeth and Banquo.

Internal conflict is also sometimes introduced – conflict within the hero himself or herself: self-doubt, dilemma, uncertainty. Sometimes such internal conflict also develops among the various other 'good' or main characters.

Important point

Conflict can be external – between characters or between values and character(s) or it can be internal, a character in conflict with him/herself.

Worked example

Let's take an example from the ways in which Arthur Miller establishes conflict in *Death of a Salesman*.

In *Death of a Salesman*, the use of setting to establish conflict is made clear in the stage instructions: onstage is the salesman's house, with 'towering, angular shapes, behind it, surrounding it on all sides'. The word 'towering' suggests dominance, control, buildings that are overbearing, dwarfing the salesman's house; and 'angular' suggests sharpness, awkward and unpleasant shapes. In other words, right from the beginning we get the impression that Willy is dwarfed by an overbearing, monstrous setting over which he has no control. Miller achieves at a stroke the implications of the physical setting, while suggesting its symbolic significance. In other words, the seeds of conflict are already sown just by the scenery as the curtain opens.

Miller also makes sure that you know about the lighting to be used: the 'blue light of the sky falls on the house and forestage', but 'the surrounding area shows an angry glow of orange'. What does the blue light suggest, given that it's the light from the sky? Or does the colour 'blue' suggest loneliness and despair? Is there any significance in that blue light being juxtaposed with the 'angry glow of orange' from the surrounding area? That Willy and his family are isolated? That they are surrounded by threat and danger ('angry orange glow', where the colour orange symbolises a warning)?

The stage instructions go on: surrounding the 'small fragile-seeming' Lomans' house is a 'solid vault of apartment houses', again reinforcing the idea that their house is flimsy, insubstantial, with the contiguous apartment houses unyielding

(continued)

and sturdy. Miller uses the word 'vault' with its connotations of a tomb or burial chamber. Are those associations with death a form of foreshadowing?

The conflict, having been established, is then developed by the actual appearance of Willy. Bear in mind that the appearance of a character can also be symbolic, as is the case here. Willy enters, he is 'past sixty years of age', comes into the kitchen and 'thankfully lets his burden down'. Is there significance in calling his sample cases a 'burden', with its connotations of something that weighs you down, an encumbrance, a problem? Does that very gesture onstage suggest conflict, especially conflict within Willy, who seems to be burdened by something that bothers and exhausts him? From the very beginning, by his movements and the way he 'lets his burden down', we can deduce some kind of inner turmoil, some kind of internal conflict.

Willy returns from his unsuccessful sales trip, his 'exhaustion apparent', carrying his cases, his burden, into the living room; he then goes to the bedroom and sits on the bed beside Linda, his wife. The focus is now on the two of them.

Important point

Note, in the paragraphs above, the ways in which quotation is woven into sentence structure. A statement or claim is made, followed by a supporting quotation or textual reference. The entire quotation or just some words from it are then carefully analysed.

Important point

Be as aware as possible of the symbolic significance of character as well as setting – ask yourself in what ways is the symbolism representative of theme?

The conflict is now further established by the dialogue between the two of them. Obviously, with plays, dialogue is an essential part of the exposition and the development of conflict. Examine how the conflict is established between Willy and his wife, Linda. It tends to be one way, though, simply because she does everything to prevent argument even although he argues with each point that she makes.

When she sees him, she asks if something happened, but he replies 'with casual irritation' that nothing happened. She asks if he feels well, and he replies, somewhat ironically 'I'm tired to the death' (it's ironic in that he uses this as a cliché, without realising the significance for him of the remark). He tells her about how, when driving, he wanders off the road. But his illusions are never far from the surface as he claims that he is 'vital in New England' and that 'If old man Wagner was alive, [he'd] be in charge of New York now!' These comments are clearly at variance with his appearance and behaviour, and they form part of his inner conflict.

But also examine the contradictions he makes – for example, about the car's windshield and then about Biff. He exclaims: 'Biff is a lazy bum!' but a few lines later he avows: 'There's one thing about Biff – he's not lazy'. What do these contradictions say about his state of mind?

When it comes to characterisation, the incident about the cheese is highly illuminating:

> Linda: Willy, dear, I got a new kind of American-type cheese today. It's whipped.
>
> Willy: Why do you get American when I like Swiss?
>
> Linda: I just thought you'd like a change –
>
> Willy: I don't want a change! I want Swiss cheese. Why am I always being contradicted?

The dialogue undoubtedly illustrates conflict on Willy's part, but what is also interesting is that he makes clear that he doesn't want a change. He is unable to adapt to change, especially to the new America. The scene, later on, between Willy and Howard, involving the wire recorder, develops his antipathy towards change. Willy is in conflict with the forces of change.

The turning point

The next structural stage is the turning point of a novel or play. It is invariably the scene during which the action of the story 'turns', where the narrative changes direction, where the fortunes or fate of the main character alter, where we get a glimpse of the probable outcome of the narrative. The turning point can also be when an action of the main character can cause a downward spiral or even the death of others. It is usually the pivotal scene, the scene about which everything turns or starts to unfold.

When it comes to the play or novel that you are studying, it may not be immediately obvious which scene forms the turning point, but make sure that you know what you are looking for: (a) the point at which the 'wheel of fortune' begins to turn (b) where the descent towards the inevitable ending begins to take shape.

> # Important point
>
> Remember in English no opinions are carved in stone: it is up to you to decide which scene is the turning point. What matters is your ability to argue your case, using textual reference as an illustrative support for your argument.

You should also keep in mind that you are looking for (c) a scene which changes for the worse the main character's fortunes; and (d) a scene where at least one of the main characters understands or learns or realises something important that is usually distressing or disturbing. Be prepared then to relate the disturbing nature of this scene to your overall understanding of the play.

Worked example

In *Under the Skin* by Michel Faber, the turning point is the scene in Processing Hall (second part of Chapter 10), where Isserley witnesses the removal of her latest victim's clothes, then his tongue and his testicles. After his ordeal is over, she pleads to see one of the 'monthlings' being processed – i.e. butchered and made ready for dispatch. She witnesses the monthling being electrocuted (in the same way as we electrocute cattle) and his throat being slit (in the same way that we drain pigs of blood).

This scene is the turning point because, from this point onwards, Isserley seems to lose control; after this scene she seems no longer in charge of events, rather she seems to allow events to take control of her.

The climax
The climax of a narrative is the final point in the narrative that eventually leads to the ultimate demise of the main character (if the text is a tragedy) and to the resolution of the conflict and the theme(s). In comedies the climax often leads to a happy resolution of the conflict.

The word 'climax' ought not to be confused with the most exciting part of the story. The term 'climax' used about a narrative is a technical term referring to the point at which the protagonist (the main character and/or the person representing good and virtue) is killed, though the antagonistic forces are themselves (usually) destroyed by his death. The climax in a tragedy is the point at which nothing worse can really happen to the protagonist or main character.

First of all, when considering the climax of a play, you should try to identify the ways in which the dramatist has built tension, culminating in the climax. Think about the thematic and dramatic significance of the scene. Does the scene resolve the themes, the concerns, of the play and in what ways is the scene dramatic? When you are asked about dramatic scenes, think of dramatic irony as well as emotion and/or tension.

Important point

With literary criticism there is no right or wrong. In any given novel or play, it's possible to argue for different scenes to be the turning point or the climax. What matters is your ability to present an argument, to make a case for any given scene to be the turning point or the climax or the resolution or the dénouement, as long as you present relevant and convincing evidence drawn from the text.

Important point

Dramatic irony is when at least one person onstage isn't aware of something significant, though the audience is fully aware. For example, when King Duncan in *Macbeth* says of Macbeth's residence – 'This castle hath a pleasant seat. The air / Nimbly and sweetly recommends itself / Unto our gentle senses' – Duncan is clueless that he is about to be murdered there, though the audience is aware of what is about to happen.

Worked example

In *The Great Gatsby* by Scott Fitzgerald, the climax has to be the killing by the demented Wilson of Gatsby in his swimming pool. Death has to be the very worst that can happen. From that point onwards, we are faced with the resolution to the theme(s) and the final dénouement.

Important point

You should by now have worked out which scene is the turning point and which the climax of the texts you are studying.

The resolution

The resolution scene is the point at which the conflict between the hero and the antagonist becomes disentangled, thus resolving the issues.

Important point

Be sure that you open up all the possibilities of a critical essay question. Any turning point is bound to be, for example, disturbing or moving or having tragic consequences since it marks the beginning of the demise of the main character. If, then, you are asked about such a scene, consider the turning point as a possibility for your answer.

Worked example

Let's consider *Othello*. What constitutes the concluding scene? Is it when Othello kills Desdemona? Or is the killing of Desdemona the climax, in which case, the resolution and the dénouement are what follow. The scene when Othello kills himself must be the resolution, since it resolves his jealousy among other themes of the play.

The climax has to be the point at which Othello smothers Desdemona – that is the point where the worst has certainly happened to Desdemona and, arguably, where the worst has happened to Othello. Iago's duplicity has finally worked its greatest evil, compelling Othello to end Desdemona's life.

By the point of resolution all the central characters – with the exception of Iago – are dead: Desdemona, Roderigo, Emilia and Othello. The Duke appoints Cassio as the new governor, thus completing the dénouement and restoring normality.

Dénouement

The dénouement is the point at which the other characters return to a different but more 'normal' way of life. You must realise by now that the climax, resolution and dénouement can almost run into one another.

Worked example

In Arthur Miller's *A View from the Bridge*, for example, the resolution must be the death of Eddie, after which the events slip almost indiscernibly into the dénouement, the return to some kind of normality, delivered appropriately by Alfieri. In any tragedy, at the end, the dénouement, the audience should feel a sense of waste, a feeling that the main character had enormous potential, but was let down by a 'tragic flaw' or *hamartia*, often thought of as deliberate or accidental transgression, or even poor judgement, on the part of the main character.

In Eddie's case, the audience is left to make up their own minds, though Alfieri's closing speech points them in a certain direction:

> ALFIERI: Most of the time now we settle for half and I like
>
> it better. But the truth is holy, and even as I know how
>
> wrong he was, and his death useless, I tremble, for I confess
>
> that something perversely pure calls to me from his
>
> memory – not purely good, but himself purely, for he
>
> allowed himself to be wholly known and for that I think
>
> I will love him more than all my sensible clients. And yet,
>
> it is better to settle for half, it must be! And so I mourn
>
> him – I admit it – with a certain ... alarm.

Although Alfieri does state unambiguously 'I know how wrong he was', thus acknowledging Eddie's *hamartia*, nevertheless he adds that 'something perversely pure calls to me from his memory – not purely good, but himself purely, for he allowed himself to be wholly known ...' His remark 'I know how wrong he was' makes

(continued)

clear Eddie's error of judgement (if that is what it was), but by adding 'something perversely pure calls to me from his memory' he is acknowledging another side to Eddie, a good side, though the oxymoron 'perversely pure' makes the meaning less clear. Perhaps Alfieri means that Eddie's desire to show Catherine avuncular goodness is too defiantly pure, too unyielding, or even that because it wasn't so obvious at the time it is only now apparent when Alfieri recalls his memory.

Significantly, he repeats his opening remark: 'it is better to settle for half'. Alfieri points out the other aspect of Eddie's error of judgement, but he also points out the tragic waste. His death, he says, was 'useless', it achieved nothing, and although Alfieri mourns him, he does so 'with a certain ... alarm'. Is he indicating a world that will increasingly not settle for half, but will increasingly resort to violence and death?

When it comes to preparing your play (or novel) for the examination, check that you know how the writer has used the following techniques:

- Characterisation – how the characters have been established in the exposition and developed later;
- Setting – how the writer used setting in time and place and how the setting relates to theme;
- Stage directions – see pages 61 – 64.

Symbolism

You should also consider a writer's use of symbolism to help establish any of the above.

Let's examine Chapter III of *The Great Gatsby*.

Worked example

Chapter III of *The Great Gatsby*, where Nick Carraway describes the quantities of food for Gatsby's weekend parties, along with the waste afterwards:

On week-ends his Rolls-Royce became an omnibus, bearing parties to and from the city, between nine in the morning and long past midnight, while his station wagon scampered like a brisk yellow bug to meet all trains. And on Mondays eight servants including an extra gardener toiled all day with mops and scrubbing-brushes and hammers and garden shears, repairing the ravages of the night before.

Every Friday five crates of oranges and lemons arrived from a fruiterer in New York – every Monday these same oranges and lemons left his back door in a pyramid of pulpless halves. There was a machine in the kitchen which could extract the juice of two hundred oranges in half an hour, if a little button was pressed two hundred times by a butler's thumb.

The extract is full of symbolic significance. First of all, there are the references to cars, representing the new consumerist America, with his Rolls-Royce becoming an omnibus (the earlier word for 'bus', suggesting carrying lots of people), indicating the sheer numbers attending; 'his station wagon scamper[ing] like a brisk yellow bug', indicating again the need to transport many people. There is also Fitzgerald's use of the colour yellow, symbolising wealth.

In addition, the 'eight gardeners' and the polysyndetic list of all that they do – 'with mops and scrubbing-brushes and hammers and garden shears, repairing the ravages of the night before – conveys the relentlessness of the work and the doggedness required of the gardeners, all building up to the climax of 'the ravages of the night before', where 'ravages' conveys the extent of the damages and destruction caused by Gatsby's guests. Others are left to clear up the mess, the waste created by the wealthy.

But it is in the next paragraph that Nick so effectively conveys the sheer extravagance and volume of waste produced by the vast consumption of alcohol and food at the parties. The five crates of oranges and lemons that arrive from the fruiterer in New York (again suggesting expense) leave on the Monday by the 'back door in a pyramid of pulpless halves'. That they leave by the 'back door' suggests the need to conceal the nauseous waste and unpleasantness, while the alliteration of the harsh 'p' (plosive) sound, along with the sheer volume suggested by 'pyramid' in 'pyramid of pulpless halves', makes clear the extent of the waste produced. The Friday arrival of the fruit and the disposal of it every Monday symbolises the lavish costs as well as the extravagant waste produced by Gatsby's parties.

Scottish texts – drama and prose

In this chapter, we will deal with the approaches to Scottish prose and drama texts and to the exam questions themselves. The Scottish text section is worth 20 marks, the equivalent of 20% of the marks available for Higher English.

In the Scottish text section, you have to choose a set of questions for each specified drama *or* prose text *or* a set of questions on one of the poems from the list of specified poets. In this chapter, you will find out how to tackle the various 2–3-mark questions and the final 10-mark question.

The Scottish text section demands that your approach to the study of these Scottish texts will be different from the study of your texts for the critical essay. You still need to know about the themes of all the texts you are studying and about the techniques by which those themes are portrayed by the writer, but this will be at a much more detailed level.

The Scottish text questions are, in effect, a combination of textual analysis questions concerning the given extract/poem, along with the 10-mark question, which could be about the way themes, character development, setting, symbolism or literary or linguistic techniques are deployed throughout aspects of the whole text or throughout other of the specified poems.

Worked example: drama

Let's put all the above into practice by looking at a particular example. Read very carefully the following extract from *Men Should Weep* by Ena Lamont Stewart:

GRANNY: Aye … that's a I'm fit for noo! Sittin an gantin.

MAGGIE: I wish ye could pit yersel tae bed. Ye're as much

bother as anither wean.

GRANNY: That's right, cest up whit ye're daein for yer man's aul

mither! (*Whining and rocking*) oh, it's a terrible thing

tae be aul wi naebody wantin ye. Oh, it's time I

wisna here!

MAGGIE: Time I wisna here tae; I should be reddin up the place

a bit afore Lily comes. Right enough, if a woman did

everythin that ought tae be done aboot the hoose,

she'd go on a day an a night till she drapped doon

deid.

GRANNY: Eh? Whit's that, Maggie? Wha's drapped doon deid?

MAGGIE: There's naebody drapped doon deid, Granny;

Leastways, *no here*. You'll no drap! You'll just sit it

oot like it was a second roon o the pictures.

GRANNY: I'll be away soon. (*Nodding her head*) Aye. It'll no be

lang afore I'm awa. Aye. Ma lif's ebbin. Ebbin awa.

MAGGIE: Och, it's been ebbin ever since I met ye; but the tide

aye seems tae come in again.

GRANNY: (*Setting up a terrible wail*) Oh, that's no nice! That's

no a nice thing tae say! But I ken the way it is,

(*continued*)

Maggie; I'm just an aul nuisance, takin up room. I'll awa back tae Lizzie's the morn. (*Sets the chair rocking fiercely and cries*)

MAGGIE: Ye're no due at Lizzie's till the end o the month and she'll no take ye a day sooner

GRANNY: Oh, I'll no bother ony o ye. I'll awa tae the poorhouse an John can hae me boxed and buried frae there. It's him the disgrace'll fa on, no me.

MAGGIE: Och, Granny, stop yer nonsense! Ye ken fine there's nae such a thing … leastways it's got a fancy name noo. Onyway, John and me wad never send ye onywhere.

GRANNY: Ye send me tae Lizzie's

MAGGIE: Aye … well … Lizzie's tae tak her turn.

At your preparation stage for the Scottish text question, don't try to second-guess what any of the Scottish text exam questions might be. At this stage, you should undertake a thorough close analysis of your chosen text, deciding about theme and the techniques, including tone, used by the dramatist. If you undertake this process properly, then you will be able to handle any individual question that may arise in the exam.

Close analysis

In this extract, there is a kind of confrontation taking place between Maggie Morrison and her mother-in-law, known as Granny.

This scene is at the very beginning of the play, thus forming part of exposition. It introduces us to these two characters, though the focus is mainly on Maggie. Her tone is sardonic, even sarcastic. As you know, it is not enough just to make a claim that the tone is humorous – you have to support that claim by detailed textual reference and analysis.

> **Important point** !
>
> Sarcasm is stating the opposite of what you mean in order to ridicule. Sardonic humour is similar but with less ridicule, more poking fun at the person involved.

Wherein, then, does this humorous tone lie? Not with Granny, who seems at this stage to do nothing much but moan. But examine carefully how Maggie responds to her. Granny complains that all she is good for is 'Sittin and gantin'. Given that 'gantin' means wasting away, gaunt, then Granny clearly feels neglected and sorry for herself, but Maggie shows no sympathy for her, replying that she is 'as much bother as anither wean'.

Maggie feels overburdened, with little help from anyone; she claims, for example, that if a woman did everything that ought to be done, she would eventually '[drap] doon deid'. The humour lies in Granny's response of 'Wha's drapped doon deid?', clearly indicating her deafness as well as confirming that she is 'gantin'; it also indicates Granny's awareness of her own mortality.

> **Important point** !
>
> To appreciate Maggie's remark, you need to know that in the 1930s, when the play is set, picture houses showed films in 'continuous performance': that is, you couldn't book seats, and cinema goers knew that after one performance the films were repeated continuously. That way, you could turn up at the cinema (picture house) at any time, assured that you would see the film, even if you arrived when it was half-way through. It was therefore possible to see the same film twice.

But the humour is intensified when Maggie develops Granny's response, suggesting that she won't die, she'll 'just sit it oot like it wis a second roon o the pictures'. That is, she won't make her 'exit', but will sit on for a second round, watching the film again. By saying that Granny will 'sit it oot', Maggie is suggesting that Granny is passively disengaged from her existence.

(continued)

Again, Granny's next comment reveals not only her obsession with death but also the extent to which she feels sorry for herself: 'I'll be away soon. (*Nodding her head*) Aye. It'll no be lang afore I'm awa. Aye. Ma lif's ebbin. Ebbin awa.' She doesn't really believe that she is about to die, but she wants sympathetic attention from Maggie, who refuses to give in – 'Och, it's been ebbin ever since I met ye; but the tide aye seems tae come in again'. Maggie plays on the image of the figurative meaning of the word 'ebbin', thereby suggesting that Granny's gloom and self-pity can turn, like the tide, and start to 'flow', indicating that her mood can turn, becoming more cheerful.

> ## Important point !
>
> An 'ebb' tide is one where the tide is going out and a 'flow' tide is the tide coming in. Both Granny and Maggie use the image of the 'ebb' tide, metaphorically, suggesting that just as the tide ebbs and flows, so do moods and life itself.

The remainder of the scene is more about characterisation than humour, though there is still an element of play-acting on Granny's part. For example, she reacts to Maggie's comment by '(*Setting up a terrible wail*)': note that she *sets it up*, suggesting that it isn't genuine; it's more for the effect of making Maggie feel sorry for her. Granny plays the martyr role, trying to manipulate Maggie's feelings by using emotional blackmail. Obviously she doesn't believe that she is 'just an auld nuisance', but the self-pitying tone is an attempt to make Maggie feel guilty, just as the threat to go 'awa back to Lizzie's the morn' is intended to reinforce Lizzie's guilt as is the remark 'I'll awa tae the poorhouse an John can hae me boxed and buried frae there'. This is the tone of the long-suffering, self-sacrificing victim, but who has no intention of ending up in the poorhouse. She hopes that her self-pitying tone and her crocodile tears (she *cries*) will cause Maggie to become more reassuring and understanding.

But Maggie doesn't fall for Granny's dissembling (pretend emotions) and tells her to 'stop [her] nonsense'; her tangential (superficially relevant) remark that the poorhouse has 'got a fancy name noo' indicates that she doesn't take Granny seriously, and even her reassurance that 'John and me wad never send ye onywhere' is undermined by the closing line: 'Aye … well … Lizzie's tae tak her turn'. She doesn't let Granny's behaviour make her feel guilty or cause her to change her mind.

The scene, then, establishes right at the beginning of the play some aspects of both these characters. Maggie shows a strength and an insight that is going to be developed as the play progresses. Granny is a kind of foil for Maggie's wit.

But, you ask, what *kind* of questions might arise in the exam?

You could be asked, for example:

> **Q** By referring closely to the dialogue between Maggie and Granny in lines 1–20, explain what is revealed about Maggie's attitude to Granny at this stage of the play. (3 marks)

Marking instructions

Always, always note the number of marks available, because there is a formula for mark distribution. In this case you are expected to make 3 comments on 3 references – 1 mark for each appropriate comment, supported by textual reference: i.e. 1 + 1 + 1 = 3. A more penetrating comment could attract 2 marks, though there must always be appropriate references. There are no marks available for mere reference to the text.

Any of the following comments, supported by appropriate references, can make up a total of 3 marks:

'Ye're as much bother as anither wean' – Maggie sees Granny as a burden who does little to ease her workload (1 mark); she's as dependent and needy as a child (1 mark);

'Right enough, if a woman ... drapped doon deid' – she feels more than overworked and overburdened (1 mark), she feels that the demands of the household ('if a woman did everythin that ought tae be done aboot the hoose') are enough to bring about her early death ('till she drapped doon deid') and that Granny does nothing to help (2 marks);

'You'll no drap!' – reinforcing the point by teasing Granny (1 mark) that Granny does little to help (1 mark);

(continued)

'You'll just sit it oot like it was a second roon o the pictures' – Maggie is suggesting that Granny is lazy and is passively disengaged from her existence (1 mark); she does nothing to be actively and helpfully involved in the household (1 mark); again, there is the undercurrent of humour (1 mark);

'but the tide aye seems tae come in again' – she accuses Granny of faking her 'illnesses' (1 mark), though she is teasing Granny, suggesting that she always makes a remarkable recovery (1 mark).

Now let's look at a 10-mark question. For example:

Q Discuss the significance of the role of Granny's character. You should refer to this extract and in more detail to the play as a whole.

Marking instructions

You should be aware of the formula for the marking of this question. It is 2 + 2 + 6. That is:

(a) 2 marks are available for identifying what is referred to as the 'commonality' of the extract – you have to identify the theme, characterisation, image, setting, etcetera, as referred to in the question, along with a *general* comment about how the identified feature appears in the text (up to 2 marks);

(b) you must make at least one relevant reference from the extract, supporting the identified technique/idea/feature – in this case the characterisation of Granny (2 marks); thereafter,

(c) you have to identify from at least one other part of the text three relevant references (3 marks) + three supporting comments (3 marks, making a total of 6 marks). [The 6 marks can, however, be gained from two relevant references from elsewhere in the text with more developed supporting comment.]

Bear in mind that marks are awarded for the quality of the analysis rather than the quantity of references.

(a) Answer about commonality

The character of Granny is self-pitying, a trait that runs throughout the extract. She constantly complains about her vulnerable situation and the impact of getting older (1 mark) and her character gives an insight into the plight of the elderly at the time the play is set (1 mark).

(b) Answer discussing the ways in which the role and significance of her character, as illustrated above, are illustrated in the extract.

When asked to go to bed Granny whines: 'The nicht's ower lang when ye're aul' – her self-pity takes the form of complaining that because she is put to bed early, she feels lonely and really sorry for herself (1 mark). Moreover, the extract reveals Granny's concerns about getting old and becoming a burden when she says: 'I'll no bother ony o ye. I'll awa tae the poorhoose and John can hae me boxed and buried frae there.' The poorhouse was where many elderly people ended up because their pension was insufficient to afford anything else (1 mark).

You could, as an alternative comment on the reference, state:

The tone of she'll be 'boxed and buried frae there' is again a measure of her self-pity since she sees the future as nothing but death.

(c) The final stage of this question

It is essential to pick up on one aspect of the 2-mark section – from section (b) above. In this case, we'll base this answer on Granny's dependence on the family and her consequent worries about being deserted. We shall also deal with her self-pity as a theme established here and elsewhere in the play.

> **Important point !**
>
> Throughout these Scottish text questions bear in mind that there are no marks available merely for textual references – it is the quality of your comments that matters.

Let's set out the final stage of the 10-mark answer using bullet points, the advantage of which is that it probably stops your answer from becoming vague; furthermore, this approach makes it easier for the marker, always a good thing!

(continued)

Lizzie's dependence on the family is established in the extract when she says 'But I ken the way it is, Maggie; I'm just an aul nuisance, takin up room': she feels sorry for herself and she hopes that her self-pity will soften Maggie into saying that she is no problem and can stay. That same use of self-pity which shows her dependence is also seen at the beginning of Act 2 when she says 'I'm nae that dottled that I dinna ken I'm no wantit. I'm naethin but an aul nuisance tae Maggie and Lizzie'. This time she gets the response she hopes for from Mrs Harris who exclaims; 'Whit an idea! Yer no a nuisance at a! I'm shair they'll miss ye something terrible *when ye go'. The italicised* 'terrible', *perhaps, hints at the irony of Mrs Harris's remark.*

Her self-pity and worries about being abandoned to the 'poorhouse' are developed at the beginning of Act 2, where her feelings of being deserted are made clear by her remark: 'Eh dear! I'm deserted! Lizzie's forgot me!'. Note the use of the exclamation mark indicating the strength of her panic at being left as well as the use of word choice 'deserted' and 'forgot me', both of which convey her worries of being abandoned, combined with feeling sorry for herself.

This answer is very full (3 + 3 marks), but alternatively you could make three less developed points for 2 marks each.

Worked example: novel

As well as undertaking a close analysis of your chosen Scottish text, you must also be fully aware of its various themes. For example, *The Cone Gatherers* portrays the following themes, though you may detect others:

- the nature and importance of sacrifice
- the nature of evil
- the descent into evil
- the place of morality in a world torn apart by the forces of evil
- the role and significance of class conflict
- the nature and extent of human goodness
- the nature of evil on a microcosmic scale.

Let's choose one of these themes and examine the ways in which it is explored: the role and significance of class conflict. You should carry out this exercise with whichever Scottish text you are studying – you must be aware of themes and the techniques by which they are portrayed.

We shall look at the episode in Chapter 11, where the two cone gatherers seek shelter in the beach hut from the thunderstorm. The scene portrays and develops the class attitudes present at that time.

They decide to seek shelter in Lady Runcie-Campbell's beach hut, even although they know that it is out of bounds to them, and that they had promised not to get into any more trouble. But Calum is soaked through, and they both need shelter; therefore, to save his brother, Neil decides to enter the hut. Once inside, and having lit a fire, they hear a key rattle in the lock. As the door is flung open, with dramatic symbolic significance, there is heard 'the loudest peal of thunder since the start of the storm'. Sheila, Roderick and Lady Runcie-Campbell enter; the 'two men could not meet the anger in her face', such was her fury at their presence. Her entrance along with the peal of thunder create a significant and highly dramatic effect.

Neil did not know what to do or say. Every second of silent abjectness was a betrayal of himself, and especially of his brother who was innocent. All his vows of never again being ashamed of Calum were being broken. His rheumatism tortured him, as if coals from the stolen fire had been pressed into his shoulders and knees; but he wished that the pain was twenty times greater to punish him as he deserved. He could not lift his head; he tried, so that he could meet the lady's gaze at least once, no matter how scornful and contemptuous it was; but he could not. A lifetime of frightened submissiveness held it down.

Suddenly he realised that Calum was speaking.

'It's not Neil's fault, lady,' he was saying. 'He did it because I was cold and wet.'

'For God's sake,' muttered the lady, and Neil felt rather than saw how she recoiled from Calum, as if from something obnoxious, and took her children with her. For both the boy and girl were present.

(continued)

The dog had not stopped barking. Even that insult to Calum could not break the grip shame had of Neil. Still with lowered head, he dragged on his jacket. 'Get out,' cried the lady. 'For God's sake, get out.'

Neil had to help Calum on with his jacket. Like an infant Calum presented the wrong hand, so that they had to try again. The girl giggled, but the boy said nothing.

At last they were ready.

'I'll have to get my cones,' whispered Calum.

'Get them.'

Calum went over and picked up the bag lying beside the hamper of toys.

Neil led the way past the lady, who drew back. He mumbled he was sorry.

Calum repeated the apology.

She stood in the doorway and gazed out at them running away into the rain. The dog barked after them from the edge of the verandah.

'You'll hear more about this,' she said.

In the hut Sheila had run to the fire, with little groans of joy. From the corner to which he had retreated Roderick watched her, with his own face grave and tense.

Their mother came in and shut the door.

'I shall certainly see to it,' she said, 'that they don't stay long in the wood after this. This week will be their last, whatever Mr Tulloch may say. I never heard of such impertinence.' She had to laugh to express her amazement. 'Your father's right. After this war, the lower orders are going to be frightfully presumptuous.'

'Did you see the holes in the little one's pullover?' asked Sheila.

'I'm afraid I didn't see beyond their astonishing impudence,' replied her mother. She then was aware that Roderick still remained in the corner. 'Roderick, come over to the fire at once. Your jacket's wet through.' She became anxious as she saw how pale, miserable, and pervious to disease he looked. 'You'll be taking another of those wretched colds.'

He did not move.

'What's the matter?' she asked.

His response shocked her. He turned and pressed his brow against the window.

Close analysis

Part of your task in preparing this novel is to examine the ways in which Jenkins uses the episode and the characters to portray the depth and extent of the class barrier that existed in that part of Scotland during the Second World War. Our examination of this – or any other part of the novel – has to be in sufficient detail to provide material for answers to any questions that might appear as part of Section 1.

One technique that Jenkins uses throughout the episode is conflict: there is obviously conflict between Lady Runcie-Campbell and the cone gatherers, and there is some subtly expressed conflict between mother and son, Roderick. But note also, particularly in the first paragraph, the depth of internal conflict that Neil is suffering. Look, for example, at the second sentence – 'Every second of silent abjectness was a betrayal of himself, and especially of his brother who was innocent' – where 'betrayal' suggests his guilt and 'abjectness' suggests that such guilt brings feelings of misery, hopelessness, almost shameful self-loathing. Just before they arrived at the beach hut, Calum has reservations about using the place, but Neil argues that the worst that Lady Runcie-Campbell can do is expel them from her woods, whereas their health could suffer badly as a result of being soaked or, worse, they could die. Finally, he claims: 'We'll do no harm. Nobody will ever ken we've been in it.'

(continued)

After the entrance of Lady Runcie-Campbell, however, the cone gatherers' roles reverse: faced with Lady Runcie-Campbell, Neil displays submissiveness whereas Calum shows some defiance. However strongly Neil feels about the ways in which the upper classes behave towards the lower classes, he cannot lift his head 'so that he could meet the lady's gaze … no matter how scornful and contemptuous it was'. In front of the aristocracy, Neil capitulates (surrenders); he cannot overcome a 'lifetime of frightened submissiveness'. That is what makes him feel so guilty – the fact that he submits so easily to the aristocracy, people whom he despises.

The important point, however, is that she banishes them from the safety of the hut, and puts them out into the storm: '"Get out," cried the lady. "For God's sake get out."' They leave to brave the storm while Lady Runcie-Campbell and her two children, Roderick and Sheila, enjoy the safety and warmth of the beach hut. The incident, then, reveals Lady Runcie-Campbell's feelings of aristocratic superiority and her horror at what she sees as the arrogance and impudence of the lower classes; it also goes on to reveal Roderick's sense of justice combined with his capacity for compassion, while the scene exposes Sheila's disdain, combined with her seemingly infinite capacity for self-conceit and self-satisfaction.

The importance of analysis

But, as already stated, it isn't enough to 'claim' what the scene does, you must analyse how it does it. For example, 'reveals Lady Runcie-Campbell's aristocratic superiority and her horror at what she sees as the arrogance and impudence of the lower classes', but *how* is that effect achieved? To answer that we have to examine the language. When Lady Runcie-Campbell reacts to Calum's claim that Neil was protecting him from the cold and the wet, she 'recoiled from Calum, as if from something obnoxious': the word 'recoiled' suggests an almost instinctive reaction, a jerking back in horror at something disgusting. She sees Calum as something repulsive and objectionable, not only because of his appearance but because of his low social status. She uses the imperative: 'Get out', then repeats and intensifies it with the expression 'For God's sake', which is not being used blasphemously (a form of swearing, an insult to God) but as a plea to God to help her in enforcing her command.

Note also the repetition of her threat: 'You'll hear more about this' as well as her declaration that this week will be their last makes clear that she wants them expelled from the estate, largely because they, as lower orders, have been in her opinion insolent to her.

Later in the extract, she claims that she had 'never heard such impertinence', accusing them of being disrespectful to her position, and then she asserts that 'After this war, the lower orders are going to be frightfully presumptuous'. She predicts that the 'lower orders', a term which reveals her snobbery and pomposity, are going to be 'frightfully presumptuous', where the upper-class tone of 'frightfully' intensifies her fear that these people will have ideas above their station – she knows her position and wants the lower orders to remain in their position otherwise there will be upset in the stability of the social structure.

We also said that the scene 'reveals Roderick's sense of justice combined with his capacity for compassion', an effect which is created ironically by his mother's remark about 'how pale, miserable and pervious to disease he look[s]'. The irony lies in the fact that she does not recognise for a minute what is making him that way: his distaste for the way the cone gatherers are being treated. That he 'turned and pressed his brow against the window' is a response that 'shocked her', most probably because the act of turning away from her, suggests his disapproval of her behaviour and pressing his brow against the window suggests a longing for things to be different.

On the other hand, Sheila, we claimed, revealed disdain along with 'her seemingly infinite capacity for self-absorption and self-satisfaction'. The fact the she 'giggled' and then 'ran to the fire, with little groans of joy' expresses not only her emotional remoteness but also her absorption in her own comfort and her self-indulgence. Note that she emits 'groans of joy', like a cat revelling in its own ecstasy, oblivious to the feelings of others.

The whole scene, then, is central in that it brings to a certainty the cone gatherers' eventual expulsion from this microcosm of the world and prepares the way for Calum's death; it clarifies Lady Runcie-Campbell's entrenched attitudes to class as well as her incomprehension at her son's 'disquieting' and 'unhealthy' concern for the plight of Neil and Calum; and it also clarifies Roderick's capacity for justice and pity.

Let's examine the following 10-mark question:

Q A major theme of *The Cone Gatherers* is the role and significance of class conflict. With reference to such features as setting, characterisation and symbolism in this extract and elsewhere in the novel, discuss how Jenkins develops our understanding of this central concern.

(continued)

Setting/symbolism

By his use of setting in this extract and throughout the novel, Jenkins is able to convey the extent of class consciousness in society at that time. The novel is set in an estate where the owner, Lady Runcie-Campbell, regards herself as socially and morally superior to those who work in the estate. The beach hut is symbolic in that it is the microcosm of the world at large, the place where the conflict between the upper classes and 'the lower orders' is palpable. The scene is dramatised by 'the loudest peal of thunder since the start of the storm'. The thunder symbolises and foreshadows the peal of Lady Runcie-Campbell's anger, another kind of storm altogether.

Important point

Remember that both setting and character can be symbolic. Characters can be interesting in themselves, but they can also have a universal appeal, representing all kinds of aspects of society and/or humanity.

Character/symbolism

The working class is represented largely by Neil and Calum, the two cone gatherers. Neil believes when thinking about the landowners that he and Calum are 'human beings just like them'. He resents the unjust inequality, based on the accident of birth, that exists between the rich and poor.

The behaviour of especially Neil and Calum is very symbolic in this extract. The cone gatherers' roles now reverse: faced with Lady Runcie-Campbell, Neil displays submissiveness and Calum shows some defiance. However strongly Neil feels about the ways in which the upper classes behave towards the lower classes, he cannot lift his head 'so that he could meet the lady's gaze ... no matter how scornful and contemptuous it was'. In front of the aristocracy, Neil capitulates; he cannot overcome 'a lifetime of frightened submissiveness', whereas Calum stands his ground.

Characterisation

Despite Neil's hostility towards the upper class, nevertheless when faced with them he is unable to stand his ground; he becomes submissive and almost meek. He then develops shame and guilt at his own weaknesses. When Lady Runcie-Campbell enters the beach hut 'Neil did not know what to do or say', such was his cringing timidity in front of her.

Comment on the theme in the extract

The beach hut itself is hugely symbolic in that it, and the scene, represents the extent of class conflict. The whole scene is central in that it symbolises and foreshadows the cone gatherers' eventual expulsion from the estate, the microcosm of the world, and it prepares the way for Calum's death. It clarifies Lady Runcie-Campbell's entrenched attitudes to class; and it also clarifies Roderick's capacity for justice and pity.

The extract, however, is symbolically important because her intolerant class attitudes cause her to banish the cone gatherers from the safety of the hut: "'Get out", cried the lady. "For God's sake get out.'" They leave to brave the storm while Lady Runcie-Campbell and her two children, Roderick and Sheila, enjoy the safety and warmth of the beach hut. The incident, then, reveals Lady Runcie-Campbell's horror at what she sees as the arrogance and impudence of the lower classes. Roderick's misery at what has happened reveals his sense of justice combined with his capacity for compassion, while Sheila's disdainful criticism of 'the holes in the little one's pullover' reveals her lack of understanding of the plight of people less well-off than herself. By running 'to the fire, with groans of joy' Sheila further betrays her seemingly infinite capacity for self-absorption and self-satisfaction. Roderick's quietness is a measure of his innate sense of injustice.

Comment on the theme elsewhere in the novel

The setting is highly symbolic since this is a large estate, with a sizeable forest. It is wartime and Lady Runcie-Campbell, as a measure of her sense of duty, is sacrificing her trees for wood for the war effort. Two of the main characters, Neil and Calum, the cone gatherers, are employed to collect cones to be planted to replace the forest after the war.

At the very beginning of the novel, the narrator tells us that the landowner's mansion was located 'behind its private fence of silver firs', symbolising the barrier between the aristocracy within and the lower classes beyond. Thus right from the start class conflict is established, making clear by the words 'mansion' and 'private fence' the wealth, seclusion and solitude along with the privileges of the rich. As Neil 'stretched out from its ragged sleeve' an arm 'to pluck the sweet resinous cones', the words 'ragged sleeve' are an indicator of Neil's poverty. From a tall larch, Neil, the older brother, 'gazed at the great house with a calm yet bitter intentness and anticipation'. Not only are class differences established, but, by his attitude of bitterness and determination, so also is class conflict.

Class conflict is symbolised by the characters of Neil and Lady Runcie Campbell, who represent either side of the class divide. Such conflict, however, is developed

(continued)

throughout the novel by the differing attitudes of Lady Runcie-Campbell and her son, Roderick. The attitudes of the upper class are clarified by his father's letters from his posting in the war: the baronet wanted to 'be reassured about [Roderick's] manner of speaking to servants and the lower orders'. Any form of friendliness to such people, his father pointed out, was 'downright dangerous'. There was a feeling among the aristocracy, especially held by Lady Runcie-Campbell, that 'the maintenance of society on a civilised basis depends on [the aristocracy]'. Social cohesion, they believed, was maintained by everyone knowing his or her place in the social order and, she further believed, even though 'they [the lower orders] are our inferiors, they would be the first to admit it themselves; it is self-evident'. For one, Neil McPhie doesn't admit it and feels her equal; he assures Calum before entering the beach hut that someone had said on the wireless 'that in wartime everybody's equal'. His humanist view conflicts with her hierarchical view of the significance of the upper class. As her husband had claimed: 'It was even beyond God's ingenuity to achieve an equality that would work'.

Now try answering the question:

(a) unpack the question (concerning class conflict) and relate your findings to the novel as a whole;

(b) discuss the use of characterisation, setting and symbolism to present class conflict with relevant textual references from the extract;

(c) then, by examining elsewhere in the novel, make at least three relevant comments showing how setting, characterisation and symbolism are significant features in presenting class conflict.

How to write a critical essay on drama and prose

Now that you know about the various techniques used by dramatists and writers, we need to turn our minds to the kinds of essay questions that could be asked and how to apply our knowledge in answering them.

As you are aware, you need to choose one question, worth 20 marks, from five genres: Drama, Prose, Poetry, Film and Television Drama, Language. Your answer must be based on a genre different from the one chosen to answer Section 1 – Scottish text. You can spend 45 minutes on this question; 45 minutes on the Scottish text question.

You need to study how to 'unpack' a question to get the most out of it. One of the most effective ways of boosting your grade is to learn how to open up a question to make the most of it.

Let's take a look at a recent drama question, taken from the specimen paper:

Q Choose a play in which a central character struggles to cope with social convention or financial difficulties or family duties.

Briefly explain the reasons for the character's struggle and discuss how the dramatist's presentation of this struggle enhances your understanding of character and/or theme.

This is a question about conflict between a protagonist and his or her social, economic or familial setting.

If you have studied *A Doll's House* by Henrik Ibsen, you may rightly be delighted with such a question, especially with reference to the struggle with social convention. But what if you've studied *Hamlet*? Learn to open up terms such as 'social convention' and 'family duties'. Hamlet, for example, says at the end of Act I: 'The time is out of joint. – O curséd spite, / That ever I was born to set it right'. Hamlet recognises that he is out of tune with the social conventions of his time. The ghost has implored him to 'Revenge his foul and most unnatural murder' – after all, the murder of a brother was regarded by a Jacobean audience as supremely unnatural; that is, against the laws of nature as well as of the state. But Hamlet occupies a superior moral plane: he can only take revenge if he has proof of Claudius's guilt. Since the spirit of the age was to right wrongs by revenge (Laertes wants instantly to revenge his father's death, Fortinbras intends to revenge his uncle's), Hamlet is doubtlessly not part of that social convention.

Or take 'family duties' – one play that springs to mind is *All My Sons* by Arthur Miller. Joe Keller claims that he did what he did for family reasons – to do his duty by the Keller family – but what about *Men Should Weep* by Ena Lamont Stewart? One of the main themes of this play is the significance of the role that Maggie plays in keeping her family together under tremendous financial constraints.

(continued)

Maggie copes with abject poverty, mainly created by the sheer number of children she has to cater for, by having to look after her ageing mother-in-law, along with a husband who is unemployed.

Now let's think about prose questions. If you are asked about setting, remember that time is an important aspect of setting as well as place – in what way(s) is time an important feature of the novel you are studying? Time is as concerned about the timescale over which the novel is set as much as it has to do with when it is set.

Important point

You can use any of the listed Scottish texts for the critical essay as long as you do not answer from the same genre as in Section 1.

If you are asked about a disturbing or violent incident, think about the structures we set out on pages 58–60. Has the incident anything to do with the establishing and development of conflict or the turning point of the story? Has it to do with the climax or even the resolution? What if the question is about a central character? Need that be the protagonist? Think of all the important characters and choose the one who best fits the question. This could be a minor character – all novels to some extent present minor characters whose role is maybe to act as a foil to the main character(s) or, perhaps, it is to reflect/change/challenge aspects of the main character's role in the novel (or short story). Questions tend to be about the exposition of a piece of fiction or the turning point or the climax. It can also be about the satisfactoriness of the resolution and/or dénouement.

Since questions can also be about symbolism, remember that setting and characters can be representative of aspects of the theme of the novel or short story. Setting and character can be of particular interest – are interesting in themselves – or they can be of universal interest, in that they comment on some aspect of the human condition.

Important point

Remember to number your answer (in the margin) to correspond with the question number in the paper.

And, of course, questions can be about diegesis (a word often used about film narrative), which means the way(s) in which a narrative is related. Check pages 52–56 to remind yourself of narrative point of view. *The Great Gatsby* and *The Kite Runner* are excellent choices for questions about narrative structure.

Let's have a look at the following question from the drama section:

Q Choose a play in which conflict between two characters is an important feature.

Briefly explain the nature of this conflict and discuss how the dramatist's presentation of this feature enhances your understanding of the play as a whole.

Note that the question is in two parts: (a) you are asked *briefly* to explain the nature of the conflict, and then (b) you have at greater length to show how the dramatist's presentation of the conflict enhances your understanding of the play – i.e. your understanding of the theme. You can either deal with these two aspects separately or together, each as part of your line of thought.

Several plays come to mind: *Hamlet* (Hamlet and Claudius), *The Crucible* (John Proctor and Parris/the court/the social mores of Salem at the end of the seventeenth century), *All My Sons* (Joe Keller and Chris), *A Streetcar Named Desire* (Blanche DuBois and Stanley Kowalski), *A View from the Bridge* (Eddie Carbone and Rodolpho/Beatrice/the mores of Red Hook in the 1950s), *Othello* (Iago and Othello/Cassio)

It is important to remember that you can open up the question: for example, you can treat the mores/attitudes/prevailing moral environment as a character. In *A View from the Bridge*, the use of symbolism helps convey the conflict. For example, the bridge spans two very conflicting communities – the poverty of the Brooklyn neighbourhoods filled with ethnic labourers on the one hand and international, sophisticated Manhattan on the other with its institutions and lawyers. Moreover, the bridge also spans family/community taboos, associated with European tribal loyalties embedded in immigrant culture with the system of the laws of the United States.

In *Othello*, too, apart from the characters themselves, there is the conflict, symbolically presented, between the sophistication of Venice and the chaos of Cyprus, the one not understood by Othello while the other sees his downfall.

(continued)

Detailed plan for an essay on *A Streetcar Named Desire*

Introduction

The first step to take in your critical essay is the naming of the text and the author, both embedded in an opening sentence that uses the wording of the question. Since we are basing the answer on *A Streetcar Named Desire*, you must name the play and the author, Tennessee Williams, followed by the words of the question:

> **Important point !**
>
> You have to produce a line of thought or argument, based on the question. Make sure that you have a line of thought throughout and not just a series of random points.

In order to convey the theme of his play, *A Streetcar Named Desire*, the dramatist, Tennessee Williams, creates conflict between Blanche DuBois and Stanley Kowalski, two characters opposed to each other in many ways.

As part of the introduction you should also indicate your 'agenda', the techniques you consider to be important in conveying the theme:

In order to convey the theme of his play, 'A Streetcar Named Desire', the dramatist, Tennessee Williams, creates conflict between Blanche DuBois and Stanley Kowalski, two characters opposed to each other in many ways. Williams uses these characters as representatives of the opposing nature of certain American values current at the time of the setting of the play in the 1940s.

It is clear then from this introduction that you are going to deal with the techniques of characterisation, symbolism and setting. You can deal with each of these separately but an integrated, cohesive answer will appear more considered.

Have a plan

1. The introduction as above.
2. Some background concerning the two characters – also refer to stage instructions.
3. Next you have to show the nature of the conflict by referring to setting and an example that illustrates your point.
4. Then deal with the development of the conflict – again with textual reference.
5. Introduce the idea about character as representation:

In many ways, Stanley is the symbol of aspects of the American dream. He loves America. He may be of Polish descent, yet he detests the idea of being Polish and scolds Blanche for calling him Polack because he sees himself as American: 'I am not a Polack ... But what I am is a one hundred percent American, born and raised in the greatest country on earth and proud as hell of it'. Blanche, on the other hand, represents the gentility of the American South. The Southern states retained many of their old values, and remained what was considered to be old-fashioned: conservative, family-orientated, civilised, though their previous successes were undoubtedly due to a slave-driven economy. Stanley, working class, alpha male, sexist, brutal in many ways, the representative of the working-class North, triumphs over the South – made clear by the 'rape' scene. He has ensured that Blanche is not only isolated from society but is expelled from it. The modern Northern attitudes of materialism and industrial success triumph over the old-fashioned Southern values of polite gentility and sensitivity.

6. Conclude your essay by briefly drawing together the ideas you have set out.

> **Important point**
>
> Make sure that from time to time you refer back to the question – thus ensuring that you remain relevant; use words such as *since, thus, hence, clearly, similarly* at the beginning of the paragraph to help indicate that you are proving a case.

> **Important point**
>
> Plan your material appropriately – ensuring that your answer will cover all aspects of the question asked; you have 45 minutes, leaving plenty of time for a 5-minute plan – it will help you stay focused and remain relevant.

Your plan does not need to be as detailed as the one above, but do sketch out ideas before you begin – that way you ensure you are relevant and that you stick to the terms of the question.

Finally, it is worth considering prose non-fiction: questions there can be about entire books, such as a biography, autobiography or travel books, but questions can also involve pieces of journalism or essays. Questions tend to be about the ways in which writing techniques are used to persuade or entertain or convince or enlighten or create a powerful impression or engage the interest of yourself (the reader).

Remember to introduce and conclude your critical essay effectively, paying attention to cohesion (through appropriately linked paragraphs) as well as coherence (by ensuring that your essay hangs together and is complete in itself).

Look at pages 138–142 for an example of a complete critical essay on poetry.

> **Important point**
>
> Produce a cohesive and coherent piece of prose – 'cohesive' means that it has to be well-linked and 'coherent' means that it must make sense by itself by having been appropriately introduced and concluded.

An introduction to poetry

Although the questions for the Scottish text poetry section and the critical essay section are quite different, nevertheless many of the techniques used by the poets are common.

There are specific poetic techniques: rhyme and rhythm, for example, but poets sometimes adopt a specific type of poem, such as a ballad or a villanelle, while some choose free verse. Often poets exploit the use of enjambement and employ sound. But most importantly, poems are written in lines.

Rather than deal technique by technique, here we will examine the relevant techniques as we study several poems, some from the list of Scottish texts, some that may well be useful for the poetry section of the critical essay part of the paper.

First of all, though, we need to consider themes and effects.

Themes, effects and analysis

When you read a poem for the first time, it is sensible to decide what it is about. What is its theme? Read the poem and then form an opinion about the theme.

When you are studying your chosen poems for the Critical Reading paper (Sections 1 and 2), it is also helpful to know something about the contexts in which the poems were written. A few biographical details about the poet will help you come to terms with the themes. Find out about the era in which the poets were writing – the social, political, historical, cultural contexts; the kinds of issues that each poet tended to explore; the poetic forms and structures that each preferred – traditional form, blank verse, free verse. The ways in which poets use rhythm. Such background knowledge can enable and enlighten your understanding.

The most effective way to approach poetry is to ask yourself the following three questions –

(i)   What is the poem about?

(ii) What effect(s) does the poem have on me?

(iii) How have these effects been achieved (i.e. what techniques have been used) and how do they contribute to the theme(s)?

> **Important point**
>
> These three questions can – and should – be applied to any text: drama, prose fiction, prose non-fiction, poem, film, television series, advertisement.

In other words, the first thing you have to do after reading a poem is to ask yourself what it is about or what is the issue or concern or emotion portrayed by the poem. What does the poem 'say' to you?

Next, you have to look at the techniques used by the poet to portray that theme – structure, setting, symbolism, rhyme, rhythm, sound, word choice, imagery, contrast. If the poem involves a character, then you need to include characterisation. Work out, in your opinion, which techniques are the most appropriate.

Then you have to ask yourself how these poetic techniques help convey the theme that you have decided upon.

Now let's return to the three questions above:

(i)   What is the poem about? – The answer to this question is theme. Try to answer in one or two words – e.g. the theme is jealousy, regret, nostalgia, past experiences, beauty, isolation.

(ii) What effect(s) has the poem on me? – The answer to question (ii) is your own *personal reaction*: laughter, sadness, regret; quite often we react by acknowledging that the poem recalls feelings that we have already had, or expresses ideas new to us.

(iii) How have these effects been achieved (i.e. what techniques have been used) and how do they contribute to the theme(s)? – The answer to (iii) lies in the critical analysis, practical criticism, or the **textual analysis** of the poem. In answering this question, you are engaged in the process of evaluation – examining **how** the effects have been achieved and how they contribute to the overall theme(s).

The most important of these three questions is perhaps this last one – the textual analysis of the poem. Indeed, the study of any literary or media text should use the approach of textual analysis. The study of *all* texts should be based on textual analysis.

As we study the poems for either of the two sections – Scottish poetry texts and the critical essay poetry section, we will refer back to this chapter.

It is important to remember that if you choose to deal with, say, *Sunset Song* by Lewis Grassic Gibbon or *Men Should Weep* by Ena Lamont Stewart as part of the Scottish text section (either prose or drama), then you are free to choose the poetry section of the critical essay and that means that you will be able to use the poems specified for the Scottish text poetry for the critical essay.

This means that either:

(a) you will be studying the Scottish specified poems for the Scottish text section using the approach as set out in the next chapter;

OR

(b) you will be studying a range of poems for the critical essay and the poems in the next chapter could be part of that range.

Scottish texts – poetry

We'll begin by analysing *Havisham* by Carol Ann Duffy, a poet from the Scottish poetry list for Section 1. Once you have read the poem, we'll study the various techniques used by Carol Ann Duffy in the poem.

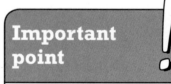

Important point

Many poetic devices will be illustrated as we deal with the following specified Scottish poems.

Worked example

Havisham

Beloved sweetheart bastard. Not a day since then
I haven't wished him dead. Prayed for it
so hard I've dark green pebbles for eyes,
ropes on the back of my hands I could strangle with.

Spinster. I stink and remember. Whole days
in bed cawing Nooooo at the wall; the dress
yellowing, trembling if I open the wardrobe;
the slewed mirror, full-length, her, myself, who did this

to me? Puce curses that are sounds not words.
Some nights better, the lost body over me,
my fluent tongue in its mouth in its ear
then down till I suddenly bite awake. Love's

hate behind a white veil; a red balloon bursting
in my face. Bang. I stabbed at a wedding cake.
Give me a male corpse for a long slow honeymoon.
Don't think it's only the heart that b-b-b-breaks.

Sometimes it is useful to talk about the 'voice' in the poem, a voice deliberately created by the poet to be different from his or her own. Sometimes, especially with Carol Ann Duffy's poetry, it is the voice of a character from a novel or a play or the voice of a character from history. In the above poem, the voice is that of Miss Havisham, a character from *Great Expectations* by Charles Dickens (1812–70), a nineteenth-century novelist. In this poem, it would be difficult to confuse the 'voice' with that of Duffy's own, but if you listen carefully you can 'hear' the persona's voice to the extent that you get a strong impression of what she was like.

First of all, you probably need some context in order to understand the poem fully.

(continued)

Context

Great Expectations is narrated by Pip, an adult who is relating his experiences as an 11-year-old boy. In the novel, Miss Havisham wears a wedding outfit, but 'the dress is yellowing' (compare with the poem *Havisham*, stanza 2, lines 3–4). The wedding, we discover, should have taken place some time ago, when Havisham had 'the rounded figure of a young woman' unlike the 'skin and bone' she is now. As a consequence of having been jilted by her fiancé on the morning of her wedding, Miss Havisham is still wearing her ageing wedding dress. She is still suffering from feelings of resentment and bitterness over a decade later.

Read the first stanza again:

> Beloved sweetheart bastard. Not a day since then
> I haven't wished him dead. Prayed for it
> so hard I've dark green pebbles for eyes,
> ropes on the back of my hands I could strangle with.

You must notice right away that this time the story is being related by Miss Havisham herself. And she is still very angry at having been jilted by her lover.

Let's examine some of the techniques used by Carol Ann Duffy in this poem.

Alliteration

The first sentence uses alliteration of the hard 'b' sound (the hard consonants 'b' and 'p' are known as plosives, the hardest sounds in the language). Also 'Beloved sweetheart bastard' is a minor sentence, thus drawing attention to its effect, and stating in no uncertain terms what Miss Havisham thinks of her lover. He is a 'bastard' but he is also referred to as her 'beloved sweetheart', a clear use of oxymoron, thus making clear her two conflicting feelings.

> ## Important point
>
> Oxymoron is the juxtaposition of terms or ideas that are contradictory. Note that the terms have to be contradictory but do not form an actual contradiction. The two terms are almost always both true.

Oxymoron

The device in 'Beloved sweetheart bastard' is called oxymoron because 'beloved sweetheart' contrasts powerfully with 'bastard': both aspects of the apparent contradiction are true – she regards this man still as her 'beloved' and her 'sweetheart', but he is also a 'bastard' for what he did to her. The alliteration of the plosives, the shortness of the sentence, the fact that it is a minor sentence, and the oxymoron all combine to make this a highly dramatic opening, which captures the reader's attention.

Important point

Note that the word 'juxtaposition' means no more than placing words or ideas side-by-side; it does NOT mean contrast.

But notice, too, that the oxymoron 'Love's / hate behind a white veil' spills over between two verses – from verse 3 into verse 4:

> Love's
>
> hate behind a white veil; a red balloon bursting
> in my face. Bang. I stabbed at a wedding-cake.

She states that behind her white veil there is 'love's hate', two words that are seemingly contradictory. The expression is an oxymoron which captures the hate that belongs to her love – because she was jilted. But also note the reference to the 'white veil' which usually hides a blushing bride, though in her case the veil masks her hatred.

The 'red balloon' is something associated with the wedding party and is symbolic of celebration, but here it is 'bursting' thus symbolising her hopes and dreams, cruelly bursting in her face. The plosive 'b' reinforces the onomatopoeic 'Bang', thus representing the noise and violence of the balloon bursting. The colour red, perhaps, signifies her anger.

(continued)

Enjambement

We have already noticed how some sentences spill over from one line to the next. The device is known as enjambement.

Here is another example:

> Beloved sweetheart bastard. Not a day since then
> I haven't wished him dead.

Note that in the middle of the line there is a full stop after the short three-word sentence, thereby creating a pause known as a caesura, which forces the sentence beginning 'Not a day since then' to spill over onto line 2. The effect of enjambement is to give priority to the sentence structure over the line structure, thereby giving the poem more of a prose-like feel, which in turn makes the poem more accessible to the reader.

But there is another effect: enjambement, because it spills over or runs on from one line to the next, also captures/represents the thoughts of the persona as they spill over or run on, thereby adding 'flow' to her thoughts, in this case representing the flow of her anger. It's as though she is working herself up by one thought running on after another, reflected by the lines running on one after the other.

It is the same with the other lines that we examined:

> Love's
>
> hate behind a white veil; a red balloon bursting
> in my face. Bang. I stabbed at a wedding-cake.

where the caesura before 'Love's' forces the enjambement between the verses. It links the verses and contributes to the build-up in violence ending in the stabbing of the wedding cake.

Sentence structure/line structure

Another effect created by enjambement is that the beginning of the next line contains a kind of surprise. Because we are dealing with lines of poetry, even although there is enjambement, nevertheless we, as readers, pause ever so slightly at the end of one line, thereby allowing the beginning of the next line to come as a bit of a surprise. Look at the pause after 'Love's', causing 'hate' to come as a shock.

Word choice

The phrase 'dark green pebbles for eyes' is particularly effective in that it not only captures the hardness of her eyes ('pebbles') but also suggests her jealousy by the use of the colour green – 'the green-eyed monster'.

By making the word 'Spinster' a minor sentence, Duffy ensures that attention is drawn to its highly pejorative (sneering) connotation. The word 'spinster', rarely used nowadays, denotes an unmarried woman, but also suggests that she is unmarried because she is unattractive. In using the word to label herself, Havisham suggests that she is now old-fashioned and unlikely ever to find someone to marry. She spends 'Whole days / in bed cawing Nooooo at the wall', an indication of her depression (staying in bed) and her despair ('cawing' like a crow, facing the wall).

As you can see, there are many examples you can choose, but one of the most effective is when she says she 'stabbed at a wedding-cake', a violent image conveying a repeated gesture ('stabbed *at*'), as she desperately wanted to destroy the wedding cake, another symbol of her non-existent wedding. Also the use of 'Give me a male corpse' suggests something sinister, as well as her desire for revenge on all men.

Capitalisation

Or rather the lack of it! The initial letter of the first word in each line (except for the beginning of the second verse) is in lower case – unlike poetic tradition. This, too, helps the poem appear more like everyday speech by making it more informal.

Rhyme and imagery

There is also a lack of rhyme, another way of making the poem less like poetry and more like prose; also the rhythm is irregular, with hints of weak/strong – the iambic

(continued)

rhythm of everyday speech. You can't help but admire the image of the 'ropes on the back of my hands' – the protruding veins of an elderly person – which she could use to 'strangle' the man who jilted her. It is only too apparent that the persona hates men as a result of what happened to her; there is no evidence at all that Carol Ann Duffy is full of hatred – only the persona!

Rhythm and sound

Although the rhythm isn't regular, Duffy does exploit it to good effect. For example, listen to the following lines from the second verse:

> Spinster. I stink and remember. Whole days
> in bed cawing Nooooo at the wall; the dress
> yellowing

Poetic rhythm is often iambic (weak/**strong**) or trochaic (**strong**/weak). But note the word 'Spinster' – it has two equal stresses (**Spin/ster**), known as a spondee. It is useful to know that word, since many dramatic effects are created by the use of a spondee. Here, Duffy, by accentuating both syllables of 'Spinster' in this one-word sentence is thereby drawing even more attention to it. Moreover, she is also accentuating the ugliness of the sound of the word, reinforced by the alliteration of the nasty 's' sound and the unpleasant short 'i' sound in the first syllable. The ugly sound supports the pejorative tone of the word, which was often used to describe an unmarried, often unattractive, woman.

These devices specific to poetry we'll refer to as poetic devices or poetic techniques, which include verse structure, rhyme scheme, line length, line endings, positioning, rhythm, sound (devices such as alliteration, assonance, onomatopoeia) as well as symbolism, contrast and, most importantly, enjambement.

What kind of questions can you expect on a poem such as *Havisham*? Let's look at the following question.

Q By referring closely to **stanza 1** analyse the use of poetic techniques to emphasise the ways in which the persona feels about her situation. (3 marks)

3 marks indicate that you need to make three comments analysing the techniques by which the persona's feelings are emphasised, though a detailed, insightful comment may well be awarded 2 marks.

Possible comments include:

The opening minor sentence 'Beloved sweetheart bastard', where the alliteration of the hard, plosive 'b' sound draws attention to and emphasises her anger; Havisham thinks that her lover has been brutal and heartless. The word choice 'bastard' conveys her hatred but since she also refers to him as her 'beloved sweetheart', she still thinks softly of him. The expression is an oxymoron, which makes clear her two conflicting feelings. [An insightful comment worth 2 marks.]

'Not a day since then' conveys the period of time that she has been jilted, which also emphasises not only the extent but also the duration of her anger, especially when combined with 'I haven't wished him dead'. Since there is a line break after 'Not a day since then', there is pause before the phrase – 'I haven't wished him dead' – in the next line, thus creating an element of surprise at the violence of her wish. [Also worth 2 marks.]

The word choice 'dark green pebbles for eyes' emphasises her feeling of hardness towards him – the word 'pebbles' suggests something round and hard – but also the word 'dark' describing her eyes also suggests her suffering over this period of time. Moreover, this expression further emphasises her deep-seated coldness towards him, suggested by the term 'dark green', where 'dark' has almost evil connotations. [2 marks]

The fact that she could 'strangle him' suggests the violence she feels towards him [1 mark] while the 'ropes on the back of my hands' perhaps suggests that she is now older ('ropes' referring to veins), an emphatic reference to the duration that she has suffered and felt hatred. [1 mark]

Note that you have always to refer closely to the text in support of your comments.

Worked example

As with drama and prose, poems, too, have themes.

Let's put all of this theory into practice. Read carefully the following poem, *An Autumn Day* by Sorley MacLean (1911–1996):

An Autumn Day

On that slope
on an autumn day,
the shells soughing about my ears
and six dead men at my shoulder,
dead and stiff – and frozen were it not for the heat –
as if they were waiting for a message.

When the screech came
out of the sun,
out of an invisible throbbing,
the flame leaped and the smoke climbed
and surged every way:
blinding of eyes, splitting of hearing.

And after it, the six men dead
the whole day;
among the shells snoring
in the morning,
and again at midday
and in the evening.

In the sun, which was so indifferent,
so white and painful;
on the sand which was so comfortable,
easy and kindly;
and under the stars of Africa,
jewelled and beautiful.

One Election took them
and did not take me,
without asking us
which was better or worse:
it seemed as devilishly indifferent
as the shells.

Six men dead at my shoulder
on an Autumn Day.

Versification

Right away you notice that it is written in free verse – i.e. there is no rhyme and the rhythm is irregular. But there are five 6-line verses with one 2-line verse – so there is some regularity in the verse structure. To what effect? Certainly the structure draws attention to the short, one sentence couplet forming the final verse and thereby bluntly stating the main concern of the poem.

Context

It is helpful to know that Sorley MacLean fought in the Second World War (1939–1945). He served in Libya and Egypt, though in 1942 he was so badly wounded at the battle of El Alamein (in north Egypt, on the Mediterranean coast) that he had to be discharged from the army the following year.

That piece of information helps contextualise the poem. The 'shells' that are 'soughing about [his] ears' are clearly war-time exploding shells, and the 'six dead men at [his] shoulder' are fellow soldiers who have been killed beside him in the action in North Africa. But what is the poem about? Clearly, it is about war, but that seems a bit general. It begins with the scene – it is an autumn day and the shells were 'soughing' (a rushing, swishing sound) about the persona's ears. There are 'six dead men by [his] shoulder, / dead and stiff', words which suggest that they have been dead for a long time. The word 'stiff' indicates that rigor mortis has set in; they appear 'frozen' but the persona knows that they can't be because of the heat (a kind of oxymoron?), but they also appear 'as if they were waiting for a message', which perhaps suggests that they have a look of expectation.

(continued)

In the third verse, the persona suggests the passage of time – they have been dead for the whole day, with the constant sound of the shells around him. But it is in the penultimate verse that the persona deals with the randomness of their deaths. The shells 'took them / and did not take [him]'. It was as though the whole experience was 'devilishly indifferent', a word that is repeated from an earlier verse, where he describes the sun as 'indifferent'. Is he saying something about the random nature of war or the random nature of our existence?

You need to make your own mind up about the theme of the poem – what does it suggest to you?

What kind of question on this poem might you expect? Let's examine the following.

Q By referring closely to the second stanza, analyse the use of poetic devices to convey the horror of war. (4 marks)

Here you have to make textual reference to two examples of the ways in which MacLean conveys the horror of war in stanza two. Two marks can be awarded for reference plus insightful comment, 1 mark for reference plus a basic comment. You have to make one other such reference + comment to score the 4 marks. There are no marks available for reference alone.

Here are some possible answers:

Part of the horror of war is conveyed by MacLean's portrayal of the persona's inability to see and hear the direction of the shells reinforced by his mixing of visual and auditory images: he says that when 'the screech came', clearly a harsh sound image suggesting scream and shriek, words associated with excruciating pain, it came 'out of the sun', a visual image conveying the inability to see the shells against such a strong light, also suggesting terror. [2 marks]

The use of enjambement in the first three lines of the stanza helps isolate and therefore draw attention to the phrases 'out of the sun' and 'out of an invisible throbbing', again emphasising the inability of the persona to identify the shells by sight and sound, making him vulnerable. Moreover the anaphora (repetition) of 'out of' at the beginning of each line again draws attention to his inability to identify by means of vision or hearing. The synaesthesia (mixing of the visual and auditory senses) of 'invisible throbbing' surprises the reader into the shock of the persona's predicament. [2 marks]

The personification of 'the flame leaped and the smoke climbed / and surged every way' conveys the ferocity and the determination of the attack by ascribing to the flames and the smoke the ability to move with the speed and dexterity and forcefulness of a predatory animal. [2 marks]

Again, the use of personification ('shells snoring') suggests either the sound of the shells or, perhaps, a false security. The polysyndeton has the effect of drawing attention to the length of time he was there among the shells snoring/in the morning and again at midday and in the evening. [2 marks]

The use of the colon at the end of the penultimate line signals the effect of the leaping and climbing and surging: 'blinding of eyes, splitting of hearing'. Also the use of the present participles 'blinding' and 'splitting' emphasises the horror of the continuing state of his inability to see and hear. He cannot escape their horror. [2 marks]

The word choice 'splitting of hearing', with its use of the repetition of the '-ing' sound creating a kind of continuity of action, emphasises the effect of the hearing of shells exploding – almost splitting his hearing in two, creating a devastating sound effect, suggesting possible damage to his hearing as well as a general disorientation. [2 marks]

Remember to refer back to the question – each of these techniques highlights the horror of war.

Worked example

Now let's look at another of the specified poems, Liz Lochhead's *My Rival's House:*

My Rival's House

is peopled with many surfaces.
Ormolu and gilt, slipper satin,
lush velvet couches,
cushions so stiff you can't sink in.
Tables polished clear enough to see distortions in.

We take our shoes off at her door,
shuffle stocking-soled, tiptoe – the parquet floor

(continued)

is beautiful and its surface must
be protected. Dust-
cover, drawn shade,
won't let the surface colour fade.

Silver sugar-tongs and silver salver,
my rival serves us tea.
She glosses over him and me.
I am all edges, a surface, a shell
and yet my rival thinks she means me well.
But what squirms beneath her surface I can tell.
Soon, my rival
capped tooth, polished nail
will fight, fight foul for her survival.
Deferential, daughterly, I sip
and thank her nicely for each bitter cup.

And I have much to thank her for.
This son she bore –
first blood to her –
never, never can escape scot free
the sour potluck of family.
And oh how close
this family that furnishes my rival's place.

Lady of the house.
Queen bee.
She is far more unconscious,
far more dangerous than me.
Listen, I was always my own worst enemy.
She has taken even this from me.

She dishes up her dreams for breakfast.
Dinner, and her salt tears pepper our soup.
She won't
give up.

As always, we'll begin with theme, which, after careful reading, you will identify as
the persona writing about her partner's mother. Often it is the girl's mother who

is the butt of mother-in-law jokes, yet more often it is the boy's mother who causes the problems! In this case the persona, on a visit to the boy's mother's house, sees the boy's mother as her rival – or maybe it is the boy's mother who has that perspective.

Structure

The use of the title is interesting; note how Lochhead uses it as part of the first line of the poem – 'My rival's house / is peopled with many surfaces' – forming one sentence. It is very important to pay attention to the titles of poems, and here the effect is to draw the reader instantly into the poem itself.

In all, there are six verse paragraphs – since the poem is in free verse, it's probably better to refer to the verses as verse paragraphs – all of varying lengths. Note that there is a rhyme scheme, but it is almost hidden and is irregular. If you read the poem in sentences rather than lines, then the rhyme is easy to miss, especially the rhymes of the last five lines in the third verse:

Silver sugar-tongs and silver salver,	*a*
my rival serves us tea.	*b*
She glosses over him and me.	*b*
I am all edges, a surface, a shell	*c*
and yet my rival thinks she means me well.	*c*
But what squirms beneath her surface I can tell.	*c*
Soon, my rival	*d*
capped tooth, polished nail	*e*
will fight, fight foul for her survival.	*d*
Deferential, daughterly, I sip	*f*
and thank her nicely for each bitter cup.	*f*

} para-rhyme

(continued)

Some are straightforward rhymes such as 'tea' and 'me', but others are para-rhymes or half-rhymes, such as 'sip' and 'cup'. We obviously have to ask: what is the effect of such a rhyme scheme? Para-rhyme or half-rhyme creates a feeling of discomfort, almost disharmony, which in this case captures the persona's feelings of awkwardness in the presence of her mother-in-law.

Rhythm

The rhythm, too, is irregular: listen to the rhythm of the first six lines:

Silver **su**gar-**tongs** and **sil**ver **sal**ver,	*a*
my **ri**val **serves** us **tea**.	*b*
She **glo**sses **o**ver **him** and **me**.	*b*
I **am** all **ed**ges, a **sur**face, a **shell**	*c*
and **yet** my **ri**val **thinks** she **means** me **well**.	*c*
But **what squirms** be**neath** her **sur**face **I** can **tell**.	*c*

The first line is **strong**/weak, i.e., the rhythm is trochaic and with 5 beats in the line, it is trochaic pentameter. But the next line is iambic tetrameter (4 beats in the line) as is the third line, whereas the fourth is a mixture of iambic and anapaestic rhythms. The fifth line is iambic pentameter and the sixth is a mixture, this time of iambic, trochaic and iambic again. (See page 104 for discussion about rhythm.)

So: both the rhyme and the rhythm are irregular – what is the effect? Rhyme has several uses, one of which is to draw attention to the words rhymed. In this case, 'tea' and 'me' are highlighted, as are 'shell', 'well' and 'tell'. Look also in the first verse at the effect of drawing attention to 'clipper satin' and 'can't sink in' along with 'distortions in'. If you listen closely to this last line, you'll hear the last two syllables almost rhyme (para-rhyme): 'satin' / 'sink in', 'sink in' / 'tions in', and such two or more syllable rhymes are called feminine rhymes, often associated with less serious, even humorous, verse.

Enjambement

In *My Rival's House*, many of the sentences do not 'fit' the line structure. For example, examine the second verse paragraph:

> We take our shoes off at her door,
> shuffle stocking-soled, tiptoe – the parquet floor
> is beautiful and its surface must
> be protected. Dust-
> cover, drawn shade,
> won't let the surface colour fade.

Note how there is a break in the form of a dash in the second line. There is another one in the fourth and fifth lines. A break in a line of poetry is referred to as a caesura, and it often causes, even forces, the line to 'spill over' into the next line as is the case here. As discussed above, the technique of one line running on to the next is called 'enjambement'.

But, again, what matters is not simply identifying the technique but being able to comment on its effectiveness and how it helps portray the theme. Often, enjambement makes the poem seem more like prose and therefore more accessible to the reader, and that seems to be the case here as well, especially when the first line is run on from the title. But note that there are no run-on verses, which means that each verse is a verse paragraph.

Sentence structure

There is an informality about the sentence structure – the second sentence of the poem, for example, lacks a main clause: the words 'There are' are missing, leaving the sentence

Important point

Enjambement is where a line of poetry spills over or runs onto the next line; it is usually where the sentence structure doesn't fit the line structure.

Important point

A caesura is a break – indicated by a punctuation mark – in the middle of a line of a poem. The break forces the sentence to spill over into the next line or verse.

(continued)

listing the 'surfaces' and the furniture in the mother's house. The final item in the list – 'cushions so stiff you can't sink in' – is a subordinate clause forming the climax:

> Ormolu and gilt, slipper satin,
> lush velvet couches,
> cushions so stiff you can't sink in.
> Tables polished clear enough to see distortions in.

Ormolu is a kind of gold-colour, an alloy of various metals used in the process of creating gold plating; slipper satin is a matt-finished fabric; the couches (plural) are 'lush', a word we usually associate with greenery and gardens, but 'velvet' restricts the meaning to the luxurious feel of the couches. The persona has used the list to convey not only the range and extent of the expensive items in the house but also a sardonic tone. The final sentence confirms the tone when she adds 'clear enough to see distortions in': distortions in the wood itself or distortions in the images reflected in the polished surface? Whatever, the persona is gently mocking the apparent ostentation of her mother-in-law's house.

The last sentence of the third verse has two adverbs piled up before the main clause, thereby creating the build-up to 'thank her nicely for each bitter cup', the climax to the sentence and the verse. The word 'bitter' comes as a shock, highlighted by its climactic position, conveying a deprecatory attitude rather than any unpleasant taste of the contents of the cup.

Lochhead also uses parenthesis by way of highlighting information, which is mostly sarcastic in tone: for example, in the third verse there are two parentheses – 'my rival / capped tooth' and 'polished nail / will fight' – both of which create a tone of sardonic disdain, where the word choice 'capped tooth' mocks her vanity, and 'polished nail' similarly mocks the effort she puts in to her appearance, especially when juxtaposed with 'will fight', the parenthesis forming a deviant collocation that captures the mother's vanity along with her pugnacity (tendency to aggression) to defend herself against losing her son to the persona.

Important point

A deviant collocation is a group of words that don't sit comfortably together. Such expressions are as disturbing as they are surprising.

Word choice

Lochhead also uses the connotative area of words to create effect and convey her attitude towards her 'rival', the boy's mother. In the third-last verse the expression 'sour potluck of the family' brings another dimension to the poem – the idea that none of us can escape the randomness of the family into which we are born: it is, as the persona puts it, 'potluck' and it can be 'sour'. Note the use of 'bitter' and 'sour' in the poem, suggesting that the persona feels a nastiness, a 'distaste', when in her rival's house. She avoids the word 'home', which has connotations of comfort and cosiness, which the word 'house' doesn't have.

She says that the mother is 'Queen Bee', suggesting the woman's feelings of superiority and of being in control; she is the mother 'bee' whom her hive follow. But then she says in the penultimate verse that she is 'far more dangerous than me' and she has become more of an enemy to the persona than the persona is to her.

Before we look at an actual question, you should ensure that you are aware of and can analyse and/or evaluate:

- all the poetic techniques used at the beginning of your chosen poems to establish themes;
- the ways in which the poet creates a sense of time and/or place;
- the ways in which the poet creates a dramatic impact; or even
- how the poet uses the opening to engage our interest and/or make an effective opening.

Let's examine the following question.

> **Important point !**
>
> Don't be afraid of the word 'evaluate': to evaluate a technique you first of all have to analyse it and then say the extent to which you think it is effective in creating the desired effect. Ask yourself how appropriate the techniques are in achieving the effects.

Q Evaluate how effective you find the last verse as a conclusion to the poem. Your answer should deal with ideas and/or language. (3 marks)

(continued)

You need to be able to demonstrate that you understand the term 'conclusion': you need to show how the content of the last verse continues or contrasts with the ideas and/or the language of what has come before. If in doubt, refer to pages 47-8 of the RUAE section concerning conclusions.

There are 3 marks available hence you can make three relevant basic comments, while a more detailed/perceptive comment on one example could attract 2 marks. Again, there are no marks available for reference alone.

First of all, throughout the poem Lochhead has used rhyme and para-rhyme. The para-rhyme is most noticeable in the third verse, especially the last five lines: 'rival' doesn't quite rhyme with 'nail' though it does rhyme with the last syllable of 'survival', then 'sip' and 'cup' are para-rhymes. In this poem, para-rhyme suggests the discomfiture of the awkward relationship between the persona and the boy's mother. Para-rhyme continues in the fourth and penultimate verses becoming less and less regular, with some awkward rhymes such as 'house' and the last syllable of 'unconscious'. But by this last verse there is no rhyme at all, suggesting that the relationship worsens as the meeting goes on – the last verse concludes by drawing final attention to the awkwardness of their relationship by means of rhyme or the lack of it in this one verse. [2 marks]

Throughout the poem, the setting is at times when food is served – in verse three the persona is being served tea, the mother using 'Silver sugar-tongs' and 'silver salver'. Although there is an ironic contrast between the connotations of 'silver' – ostentation and value – nevertheless there is nothing to betray the mother's underlying feelings. But, in the last verse, now set at dinner time, she 'dishes up' with its suggestion of gracelessness, while the phrase 'her salt tears pepper our soup' conveys, finally, conclusively, how the mother really feels – 'salt' suggesting bitterness and sadness, especially when used to describe her 'tears'. On the other hand, 'pepper', with its connotations of hotness and burning, suggests finally her betrayal of her anger. The last verse concludes by making the mother's true feelings explicit. [2 marks]

Alternatively, you can accumulate marks the following way:

The last verse uses three short sentences, two of which form end-stop lines while the third uses enjambement to create a conclusive effect with the idea that the mother will never give up. Since throughout the poem there is much use of enjambement, its restriction here helps to conclude the poem with its climactic effect. [2 marks]

The ideas in the last verse contrast with the way in which the mother appears in the rest of the poem. To begin with she is confident and well-presented – 'capped tooth', 'polished nail' both suggest that she takes pride in her appearance while suggesting that the falseness of the tooth being capped, and her nails being polished disguise her true appearance – while in the last verse the 'salt tears' betray her bitterness and sadness, maybe her true feelings. The last verse then concludes by revealing the truth. [2 marks]

'She won't / give up' suggests that there will be no end to the way the mother feels, thus creating an effective climax to the poem. [1 mark]

The use of enjambement in the final two lines means that the reader pauses at the end of 'She won't' and is therefore surprised by the 'give up'. It makes the reader realise that there is no end to the way the mother feels about her son. [1 mark]

The 10-mark question

In order to demonstrate how to answer the 10-mark question, let's return to *Havisham* by Carol Ann Duffy, set out on page 99.

The last question always asks you to make a comparison between the set poem and the rest of the poems by the specified poet. The nature of the question will depend on your chosen poet. The following table should make everything clear:

Chosen poet	Likely comparisons	Sample question
Burns, Robert	theme / character / language / form	From your reading of this poem and at least one other by Burns, discuss the ways in which he presents hypocrisy.
Duffy, Carol Ann	theme / character / setting / form	From your reading of this poem and at least one other by Carol Ann Duffy, discuss the ways in which she presents at least one other character. From your reading of this poem and at least one other by Duffy, show how she uses contrast to present love.
Lochhead, Liz	theme / character / language / setting / form	From your reading of this poem and at least one other by Lochhead, discuss the ways in which she uses poetic devices.
MacCaig, Norman	theme / character / setting / language / form	From your reading of this poem and at least one other by MacCaig, discuss the ways in which he uses language to present ideas.
MacLean, Sorley	theme / character / language / setting / form	From your reading of this poem and at least one other by MacLean, discuss the ways in which he uses setting.
Paterson, Don	theme / language / setting / form	From your reading of this poem and at least one other by Paterson, discuss the ways in which he uses a particular incident to have symbolic significance.

How to tackle the 10-mark question

As you can see from the table above, the 10-mark question asks you to discuss theme and/or technique, with reference to the poem set in the exam and one other of the specified poems.

Let's choose *Havisham* (see page 99) by Carol Ann Duffy.

Worked example

Q From your reading of this poem and at least one other by Carol Ann Duffy, discuss the ways in which she presents at least one other character.

The question is about presentation of character, therefore you have to choose from the list another of her poems where she presents a character. You may decide that a good poem for the comparison is *War Photographer*.

Marking instructions

The marking formula of 2 + 2 + 6 still applies to the poetry section. Keep in mind that:

(a) 2 marks are available for identifying areas of 'commonality' as per question – i.e. you need to unpack the idea of presentation of character here and with reference to another poem;

(b) 2 marks are available for reference to and discussion of the extract given; and

(c) 6 marks are available for discussion of similar references to at least one other poem – in this case *War Photographer* (and possibly *Anne Hathaway*).

(a) You have to identify the commonality, which means that you have to look for the ways in which Duffy presents, in this poem, the character of Miss Havisham and other characters elsewhere in her work, especially in *War Photographer, Valentine, Anne Hathaway* and *Mrs Midas*.

(b) Now you must refer to the extract, discussing ways in which Duffy presents the character of Havisham. The question is asking about presentation of character, which in this case is achieved by the techniques of first-person narration, short sentences to imitate the spoken word, the rhythm of the spoken word, versification, word choice, enjambement and a lack of rhyme (except for the second and last words of each verse, where Duffy uses para-rhyme). Choose a couple of such techniques and, by reference to the poem, show how Duffy uses the chosen techniques to present character.

(continued)

(c) These same techniques are used in many of her poems, especially in *War Photographer*, where she presents the character of a man who records photographically places of conflict and war zones for a newspaper. Unlike *Havisham*, *War Photographer* is related in the third person by a persona, though both poems exploit ambiguity. As with *Valentine*, *Havisham* deals with a realistic view of love and its consequences, and both have an underlying violence. You could also make reference to *Mrs Midas* or *Anne Hathaway* to show how these respective characters are presented. You must, of course, make close textual references to, say, 'War Photographer' with appropriate comment.

How to write a critical essay on poetry

Now let's consider possible poetry texts for the critical essay.

If you are studying poetry for the critical essay, then inevitably you are studying either prose or drama for the Scottish text section. That means that you are free to use any of the poems from the Scottish text poetry list. Therefore, you should read the previous two chapters, where you will find background to the study of poetry along with the analysis of several Scottish poems from the specified list.

This part of the book will look at individual poems and discuss the various poetic techniques.

Ideally, you want to choose three kinds of poems: (a) those poems which express and explore themes, (b) those which present characters, and (c) poems which present a story (narrative poems). You should also consider and research specific poetic forms, such as the sonnet, the dramatic monologue, the villanelle or the ballad, since there is occasionally a question on a specific poetic form.

Poems for the critical essay need to be studied in detail since, in answering a critical essay on poetry, you are expected to be able to make close reference to the language and form of the poem. It is important to be able to support your answer by the use of quotations.

Worked example

We shall begin with a poem that presents a character – the character of Frida Kahlo, who was born in Mexico in 1907. At the age of 18, she was involved in a collision between the bus she was travelling on and a tram. She sustained many severely debilitating injuries, as a consequence of which she had, throughout her life, in excess of 30 operations, necessitating long periods of time in hospital. She was a highly talented painter, mainly of self-portraits.

Frida Kahlo Comes to Dinner, by Christine Stickland

Frida Kahlo has come to dinner,
Late, as usual, a little drunk, as usual,
Scattering fag ash like confetti,
Partnered by her perpetual pain
Whose grim claws she wears as lightly
As the ribbons on her dress.
Undefeated, her thirst for life unquenched,
There is more energy in her hair
Than in my entire body.
The brass band of her beads and bangles
Transforms her limping steps
Into a fiesta dance, all rainbow skirts
And flashing teeth and eyes.
Frida Kahlo has come to dinner,
Though eating frankly bores her,
Gets in the way of talking, drinking,
Smoking, painting, making love.
Aware of this I give her tiny pastries,
Olives, nuts, morsels of spiced meat;
Fuel for her flame, swallowed without tasting.
Frida Kahlo has come to dinner
And the carnival never stops.
Her long hands are two kites,

(continued)

> Trailing coloured tails of laughter,
> Sketching, in the smoky air between us,
> Whole galleries of portraits.
> Frida Kahlo has come to dinner
> And is now gone, taking the party with her,
> Leaving this withered Puritan
> Faded, dusty, unbearably alone.

Frida Kahlo is a poem which (a) presents a character, (b) presents and develops several themes and (c) uses many poetic techniques, thereby making it an ideal poem to study.

We shall look at some of the themes and then examine most of the techniques used by Stickland.

Themes

(a) presentation of a lively character;

(b) presentation of a character who can overcome pain;

(c) a poem which deals with contrast;

(d) it can be regarded as a 'happy' poem or a celebratory one or even a sad one.

Narrative stance

The poem is narrated in the first person by a persona who has invited Frida Kahlo to dinner; as she relates the story, she gives a first-hand impression of Frida Kahlo's appearance, behaviour and personality.

The structure of the poem is one verse paragraph divided into four sections, each separated by the refrain, 'Frida Kahlo has come to dinner':

Section 1: her appearance;

Section 2: her lively behaviour at dinner;

Section 3:   more detail about her behaviour, including her interest in and love of art;

Section 4:   the persona's sadness after Kahlo has left.

Rhythm
The rhythm is irregular:

> **Fri**da **Kah**lo has **come** to **dinn**er,
> **Late**, as **us**ual, a **litt**le **drunk**, as **us**ual,
> **Scatt**ering **fag** ash **like** con**fet**ti,
> Partnered by her perpetual pain
> Whose grim claws she wears as lightly
> **As** the **rib**bons **on** her **dress**.

The rhythm, as you can see above, is a combination of several kinds of rhythm, which, perhaps, captures Frida's halting physical movements. There is, however, a regularity of rhythm in some lines – e.g. line 2 – achieved by the repetition of the 'as usual', thus helping to combine rhythms that are awkward with those that flow – just like Frida Kahlo. A form of contrast is achieved just by rhythm alone.

Use of contrast
The poem exploits contrast. For example, Stickland refers to Frida Kahlo as someone 'Scattering fag ash like confetti', where the fag ash, with its connotations of dirt, mess, greyness and unpleasantness, is contrasted with confetti, with its connotations of celebration, joy and great colour. The mundane and ordinary is then presented as something wonderful and exciting: similarly, Frida, someone suffering from a debilitating injury, is therefore presented as someone colourful and exciting.

Another effective simile which depends for its effect on contrast is when she says that the 'grim claws' of Frida Kahlo's 'perpetual pain' are like 'the ribbons on her dress', a contrast by which she compares a violent aspect of her pain (the 'grim claws' suggesting a predatory bird) to something pretty and feminine ('ribbons'). The use of the alliteration of the plosive 'p' sound in 'Partnered by her perpetual pain' draws attention to the violence and inescapability of the pain – it is her 'partner'.

(*continued*)

There are many other contrasts in the poem: her 'limping steps' are said to be a 'fiesta dance', where again something ugly and restricting is made to be lively and colourful, with 'fiesta' having the connotations of a carnival.

Finally, there is the contrast made between Frida Kahlo and the persona herself: the persona describes herself as a 'withered Puritan', someone whose behaviour is constrained by moral rectitude (correctness), someone lifeless and dried-up, whose attitude is one of moral superiority, though she regrets being like this; Frida Kahlo, by contrast, smokes and drinks and is incredibly lively. This contrast is reinforced by the list of words in the last line: 'faded', 'dusty' and 'incredibly alone', suggesting colourlessness, aridity and isolation – once Frida leaves 'taking the party with her', the persona becomes all too aware of her barren life and her loneliness.

There are many other examples of contrast which you should note and comment on.

Use of alliteration

Stickland uses alliteration a great deal in this poem – largely of the plosives: you have already noted 'Partnered by her perpetual pain' where the 'p' and 'b' sounds capture the violence of Frida Kahlo's pain. In 'The brass band of her beads and bangles', the use of the plosive 'b' sound on this occasion captures and draws attention to the not inconsiderable noise that

Important point

Note that the effect of poetic devices, such as sound, can depend on context

she makes as she moves. The word choice, 'brass band', highlighted by the plosive, suggests something loud and triumphal.

Use of imagery

There are many examples of metaphors, similes and personification in this poem. Personification is just another kind of metaphor – a device of comparison: personification is investing an inanimate object with the characteristics of a human or animal being, thereby ascribing human characteristics to it. We have already noted above her pain (inanimate), which is said to have grim claws (animal characteristic). The grip of the pain on her is the same as the grip of grim claws, i.e. she is grasped in a vice-like grip. The pain tears at her, sinks itself into her.

The interesting thing is that Stickland then uses a simile which compares the way in which she treats the grip of the claws to the way she wears the ribbons on her dress.

In other words, she uses a simile to convey a powerful use of contrast, but she also creates the effect of the personification, drawing attention to the power and aggression of the pain. The pain is predatory, like a lion or an eagle, and grips as savagely.

Note that we have used the same reference to make more than one comment.

> **Important point !**
>
> Note how one reference can support more than one comment: note the amount of comment that we can make from that one image above.

Use of synaesthesia

Synaesthesia is a device whereby any one sense is expressed in terms of another: for example, bright pink wallpaper (visual) being described as 'loud' (auditory).

Stickland uses synaesthesia towards the end of the poem when she says:

> Her long hands are two kites,
> Trailing coloured tails of laughter

The image 'two kites ... coloured tails' is obviously a visual image, whereas 'tails of laughter' is a sound image. The device is synaesthesia, the effect of which is to strengthen both images – the kite image and the tails of laughter image. It arrests the reader's attention and makes him/her think of the meaning.

Use of hyperbole

Hyperbole is pronounced 'high-per-bowl-lee' and is a device of gross exaggeration. The image:

> There is more energy in her hair
> Than in my entire body

is clearly an exaggeration since it is impossible for there to be more energy in hair than in a body. The effect again is to draw attention to meaning, in this case the sheer energy of Frida Kahlo.

Worked example

Let's turn to a poem with a different tone altogether.

A poem which is an excellent example of a poem suitable for a question about theme or technique, or even presentation of character, is *Mr Bleaney* by Philip Larkin (1922–1985).

Mr Bleaney

'This was Mr Bleaney's room. He stayed
The whole time he was at the Bodies, till
They moved him.' Flowered curtains, thin and frayed,
Fall to within five inches of the sill,

Whose window shows a strip of building land,
Tussocky, littered. 'Mr Bleaney took
My bit of garden properly in hand.'
Bed, upright chair, sixty-watt bulb, no hook

Behind the door, no room for books or bags –
'I'll take it.' So it happens that I lie
Where Mr Bleaney lay, and stub my fags
On the same saucer-souvenir, and try

Stuffing my ears with cotton-wool, to drown
The jabbering set he egged her on to buy.
I know his habits – what time he came down,
His preference for sauce to gravy, why

He kept on plugging at the four aways –
Likewise their yearly frame: the Frinton folk
Who put him up for summer holidays,
And Christmas at his sister's house in Stoke.

But if he stood and watched the frigid wind
Tousling the clouds, lay on the fusty bed
Telling himself that this was home, and grinned,
And shivered, without shaking off the dread

That how we live measures our own nature,
And at his age having no more to show
Than one hired box should make him pretty sure
He warranted no better, I don't know.

Theme

Sometimes, with Larkin's poems, it is better to leave thinking about theme until you have done some work on the text, mainly because Larkin usually develops theme towards the end of his poems. Clearly, though, this poem is about the presentation of the character called Mr Bleaney. We'll come back to theme later.

Structure

Use of verses and rhyme – In his poems, Larkin tends to set himself a verse structure using rhythm and rhyme as well as the length of the verses; it was almost as though he imposed these patterns, constraints even, on himself, and he certainly adhered to them. In *Mr Bleaney*, there are seven 4-line verses, each using an *a b a b* rhyme scheme. The rhythm, as always with Larkin, is complex – a mixture of trochaic (**strong**/weak) and iambic (weak/**strong**):

'**This** was **Mr** (pronounced **mis**ter) **Bleaney's room**. He **stayed** (trochaic)

The **whole** time **he** was **at the Bod**ies, **till**

They **moved** him.' $\Big\}$ (iambic)

(*continued*)

Note how Larkin's use of rhythm captures the landlady's speech patterns – the first sentence is formal, informative, declarative, where the stress comes on the important words, such as 'This' (indicating the room) and 'Blean-' and 'room'. There is then a caesura, after which the speech patterns return to iambic, the second line being iambic tetrameter (four beats) plus an extra beat which is actually part of the next line's iambic rhythm. The caesura in both lines forces the entire sentence to spill over from 'He stayed' onto the next line – 'The whole time he was at the Bodies'; and then from 'till' to 'They moved him'. The use of enjambement and the iambic rhythm have the effect of reflecting the everyday speech of the landlady.

Analysis of rhyme and alliteration
The use of rhyme is used to draw attention to certain words. The rhyme scheme is *a b a b*, and the rhymes are all full rhymes, one is in fact a repetition of the word 'know'. But Larkin's combination of alliteration and rhyme enables the establishment and development of tone. For example, in verse 5 he writes:

> He kept on plugging at the four aways –
> Likewise their yearly frame: the Frinton folk
>
> Who put him up for summer holidays,
> And Christmas at his sister's house in Stoke.

Note the alliteration of the fricative (the 'f' sound) in 'frame', 'Frinton' and 'folk' – the 'f' sound can convey an unpleasant sound, especially when combined with certain vowel sounds, such as the short 'i' sound and the long 'o' sounds: the combined sound can produce a kind of weariness. Add that to the rhyming of 'folk', another word that connotes dreariness, especially since the word suggests people of the same type (boring?), and Stoke, famous then for heavy industry and 'coal' mining, and not considered to be a lively holiday town. He spent summer holidays in Frinton, the very name sounds lifeless; it was then a run-down seaside town on the Essex coast. But it is the sound of the words, reinforced by the rhyme, that conveys the tone of loneliness and lifelessness, which, by implication, suggests that Mr Bleaney suffers a dreary, dull life.

Analysis of sound

Sound is an important aspect of poetry – and prose! The 'sound' is the sound that we make when we speak. There are, as you know, five vowel sounds in English – *a, e, i, o* and *u*. We can pronounce those vowels as in *hate, feed, pine, slope* and *cute*. The sound produced in pronouncing the vowels in this way is known as *long vowel sounds*. We can, however, also pronounce these same vowels with a short vowel sound as in *hat, fed, pin, slop* and *cut*. What is important to note is that long vowel sounds tend to be more pleasant than short vowel sounds because they are made further to the back of the throat. The repetition of a vowel sound is called assonance.

But there is more to it than that. The other letters are known as consonants and can be grouped into types of sound as follows:

Letter	Type of sound	Sound effect
b and p	plosive	hard, violent
hard c, hard g, qu and k	guttural	harsh, unpleasant, violent
d and t	dental	neutral, depends on vowel sound
f, th and v	fricative	can be unpleasant, depends on vowel sound
l, w and y	liquid	mellifluous and pleasant, but the *w* sound can be mean
m and n	nasal	usually pleasant, but can be unpleasant when adenoidal
soft c, s and z	sibilant	soporific or hissing
r	rolling	almost like a vowel

(continued)

It is the combination of the consonant and the vowel sound that creates the effect. For example, it is no accident that our most effectively unpleasant swearing words begin with the plosive *b* followed by the short vowel sound.

Use of sentence structure

We've mentioned enjambement, but look carefully at Larkin's use of lists. He uses both asyndetic and polysyndetic list structures. First the asyndetic one, part of the enjambement between verses one and two:

> Bed, upright chair, sixty-watt bulb, no hook
>
> Behind the door, no room for books or bags –
> 'I'll take it.'

You should remember from the RUAE section of this book that an asyndetic structure has the effect of portraying the range and extent of the items exemplified in the list. Here Larkin is obviously looking round the room, with the landlady present, noticing the features of the room. It's as though he is giving a haphazard impression of the items, none of which suggests comfort: 'upright chair' isn't exactly one you would sit in for any length of time, and since the 'sixty-watt bulb' is visible, there can't be any lampshade offering decoration or even a softening of the glare, while 'no room for books or bags' suggests that Mr Bleaney didn't have many possessions and certainly wasn't a reader.

On the other hand, the polysyndetic list, in the penultimate verse, but finishing in the last verse, conveys the connection between the items:

> Telling himself that this was home, and grinned,
> And shivered, without shaking off the dread
>
> That how we live measures our own nature

If he has to tell himself that 'this was home' then it couldn't have really been home, but when he does tell himself that it is home, he grins and then shivers, both unpleasant words conveying muscle movement that betrays unpleasant thoughts, reinforced by 'shaking off the dread' of the idea that 'how we live measures our own nature'. In the 1950s and 1960s, the popular idea was that nurture not nature makes us who we are, but here Larkin, somewhat controversially, is suggesting that the way we choose to live our life is an indication of the kind of person we are – Mr Bleaney had a choice and he chose to live this way. Then, of course, in the last line, reinforced by the conversational rhythm and the anti-climactic 'I don't know', Larkin betrays the notion that he is in exactly the same position! Suddenly, we are forced into re-evaluating the poem and noting the irony of the whole piece: it isn't just about Mr Bleaney's loneliness and isolation, it is also about the persona's.

Note also the way in which Larkin signals the list by his use of the colon. Always remember that punctuation helps to signal meaning to the reader.

Word choice

Note the way in which Larkin uses word choice to suggest a concrete beginning to the poem – an actual room with an actual landlady. He tells us that:

Flowered curtains, thin and frayed,
Fall to within five inches of the sill,

Whose window shows a strip of building land,
Tussocky, littered.

The 'flowered curtains' in the 1950s and 1960s, suggested old-fashioned material and the fact that they were 'thin and frayed' and fell 'to within five inches of the sill' suggests that the curtains were old and not made for this window, and that they had been neglected. That the window looked out over 'building land / Tussocky, littered' further suggests that even outside the room the area was depressing and

(continued)

neglected. Moreover, the positioning of the adjectives 'Tussocky, littered' at the end of the sentence and at the beginning of a new line draws attention to them and to their meaning, thereby highlighting the neglected look of the area.

The list that spills over from verse 2 to verse 3 we have already dealt with, but the feeling of neglect and bareness is continued in the expression:

> and stub my fags
> On the same saucer-souvenir, and try
>
> Stuffing my ears with cotton-wool, to drown
> The jabbering set he egged her on to buy.

The use of 'fags' rather than 'cigarettes' suggests a working-class, common tone, as does the 'saucer-souvenir', regarded as tacky, an object of bad taste. The 'jabbering set' was most probably a radio, given the 50s/60s setting, and 'egged her on to buy' suggests that Mr Bleaney wanted to re-direct the landlady's attentions away from him. The fact that she had told the persona all about Mr Bleaney's habits (the 'four aways' is a reference to football pools, a form of gambling associated again with the working-classes) also indicates that maybe she was obsessed by him, and he did her gardening as a form of escape.

As the poem develops, vocabulary becomes more abstract and symbolic. He talks about the 'frigid wind', 'Tousling the clouds', 'fusty bed', 'dread', 'hired box': these words all suggest in turn coldness, bleakness, neglect, fear, a rented room or a coffin. Mr Bleaney's life was bleak – notice that the first four letters of Mr Bleaney's name 'blea' form the initial sound of the word 'bleak'. It is by this point – the use of abstract words and ideas – that we begin to understand the theme of this poem, the dreariness, loneliness, isolation of a man's existence, and with the final added thought – 'I don't know' – the idea, the realisation, that, by describing Mr Bleaney's life, the persona has been describing his own, since he is now in exactly the same situation.

All in all, *Mr Bleaney* illustrates many poetic techniques and also conveys many themes, already mentioned.

The same can be said for this next poem, *Waiting Room* by Moira Andrew, a poet born in Scotland but currently living in Cornwall. This time, instead of listing the techniques, which again are legion, this poem is presented to you in an annotated version.

We will use this annotated version as the basis for writing a critical essay. We'll set out the actual essay in the next chapter.

Annotating a poem

It can be useful, when you first come across a poem, to make on-the-page annotations, noting all that you can, especially any structural points, such as versification, rhythm and rhyme scheme, as well as the connotations of word choice and deconstruction of metaphors and other literary devices. Always look closely at the title of a poem, since that can tell you so much.

> **Important point !**
>
> Once you have finished annotating your chosen poems in this way, you can then list the themes, followed by the techniques, each illustrated by a textual reference/quotation. By following this method, you are in effect making your own notes about the poems you are studying, notes which will be useful when it comes to revising the poem for either Section 1 (Scottish poems) or Section 2 (the critical essay) of the exam.

No rhyme
Irregular rhythm
Good use of sound

1. Somewhere you wait for an appointment – hospital, doctor, dentist – unpleasant.
2. Somewhere to wait before a journey – apprehensive

Waiting Room

Appearance
In a room recollecting the past
Room is packed with possessions

She waits neatly, bone-china thin,
in a room tight with memories,
claustrophobic with possessions,
rendered down from eighty years,
5   eight Homes and Gardens rooms.

Bone-china is old, expensive,
and fragile, therefore appropriate

She is very old

Allusion to magazine 'Homes
and Gardens' which means her
house was large/expensive

Personality
Metaphor suggesting she is
vandalised by age
A drink associated with her
class and generation

She waits graciously, bearing
the graffiti of age. She drizzles
sherry into fine glasses, tea
into what is left
10   of wide-brimmed wedding china.

Unsteady, weak

Like bone-china / that only
so much is left is sad.

Alliteration draws attention to
her need for biographical details
of family.

With the top of her mind
she is eager to skim off news
of the family, who married whom
and when. Names elude her. Tormented,
15   she tries to trap them on her tongue.

Short sentence after long
– draws attention to short.

Oxymoron capturing her
determination but physical
difficulty

Surprise that she smokes
Use of snake metaphor captures
size and extent of veins, drawing
attention to her old age

She waits defiantly, fumbling
to light a cigarette, veins
snaking across her hands
like unravelled knitting. A man's face,
20   preoccupied by youth, looks on.

Photograph of her husband?

Change in narration to
1st person – family member?
Waiting - 1. short time to gong;
2. Longer time for rain to stop;
3. Longer wait for winter –
symbolic of death.

We leave her, the stick a third leg,
waiting to obey the gong,
(Saturday, boiled eggs for tea)
waiting for the rain to stop,
25   waiting for winter, waiting.

No choice, institutional

Inevitability of menu
Alliteration of 'w' and repitition
of 'waiting' draw attention to
the word as does position as
last word in poem, implying
waiting for death

Moira Andrew

Themes
Change
Old age
Institutional existence
Presentation of character

'Tormented' is at the beginning of the sentence, thus drawing attention
to her difficulties in remembering names, but it is also at the end of a
line, further reinforcing the difficulties by placing the word in a position
of emphasis. Also the alliteration of the 't' and 'r' creates the sound
of her trying to vocalise the names

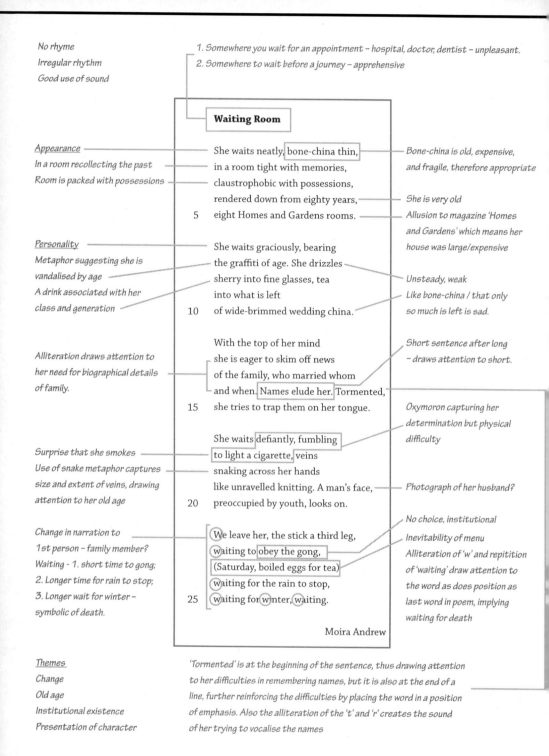

List of themes and supporting techniques

Moira Andrew uses several techniques to portray and develop the themes of *Waiting Room*. Set out for you in the table below are, in Column A, the theme being examined; Column B, a supporting textual reference; and, in Column C, appropriate, relevant analysis:

Theme	Textual reference	Connotations/analysis
Old age / waiting	The title – 'Waiting Room'	A room in which you wait for an appointment – hospital, doctor, dentist; unpleasant association. A room in which you wait before a journey – bus, railway station; associated, perhaps, with apprehension. In the context of this poem, both connotations seem appropriate as the old lady is in a room waiting to die.
Old age / change / sympathy	'bone-china thin' 'what is left of wide-brimmed wedding china'	Bone-china is old, expensive, fragile, associated with the elderly, and was often given as wedding china to former generations / the wedding china has been around for a long time, a measure of the lady's age: that only so many pieces are left is quite sad.
Old age / loneliness / isolation / sympathy / change / institutional existence	'in a room tight with memories / claustrophobic with possessions, / rendered down from eighty years, / eight Homes and Gardens rooms'	The old lady is in her room, surrounded by memories of her life; but it also contains all her worldly goods which have been reduced from everything that filled an eight-room luxury house to the one room in which she now lives – after eighty years of life. She is old and on her own.
Old age / sympathy / change	'She waits graciously, bearing / the graffiti of age'	The word choice 'graciously' suggests that she is lady-like, well-mannered, in control of herself, whereas 'the graffiti of age' suggests that her face is not only lined, but it has been vandalised, damaged, by age.

(continued)

Theme	Textual reference	Connotations/analysis
Old age / loneliness / isolation / sympathy / change / institutional existence	'With the top of her mind / She is eager to skim off news / of the family, who married whom / and when.'	Note the amount of alliteration of the 'wh' sound, drawing attention to the relative pronouns indicating her interest in the latest news of family members. The metaphors 'top of her mind' and 'skim off' suggest together that it's surface news she wants.
Old age / isolation / sympathy / change	'Names elude her.'	This short sentence after the previous long sentence draws attention to and reinforces its meaning – her forgetfulness, sometimes associated with the elderly – the implication is that she forgets the names but not the people – a form of nominal aphasia.
Old age / change / sympathy	'Tormented, she tries to trap them on her tongue.'	Note this time the combination of poetic and linguistic devices. There are two points to be made about the positioning of the word 'Tormented': it's at the beginning of the sentence and it's at the end of the line, both of which positions draw attention to the difficulties and frustrations she has in trying to remember names. Also, the alliteration and positioning of the 't' and 'r' sounds capture the effects of her trying to vocalise names.
Old age / loneliness / isolation / sympathy / change / institutional existence	'She waits defiantly, fumbling / to light a cigarette'	Interesting oxymoron – the positioning side-by-side of 'defiantly' and 'fumbling', suggesting that she is determined but hasn't the physical co-ordination to manage to light the cigarette. But the real surprise is that such a sophisticated old lady actually smokes – a sign, perhaps, of her generation, before people knew about the dangers of smoking.

Theme	Textual reference	Connotations/analysis
Old age / loneliness / isolation / sympathy / change / institutional existence	'A man's face, / preoccupied by youth, looks on.'	It may take a while to work out that this has to be a photograph of her husband – given that the 'man's face' is 'preoccupied by youth', we can infer that the photograph was taken when he was young. If that is the only photograph she has of him, perhaps he died young, killed during the First or Second World War?
Old age / loneliness / isolation / sympathy / change / institutional existence	'We leave her, the stick a third leg, waiting to obey the gong, (Saturday, boiled eggs for tea) waiting for the rain to stop, waiting for winter, waiting.'	Notice the change in point of view to first person narration: 'We'. The implication has to be that the 'we' are her family, the subject of the previous verse. That the old lady has to have a stick invokes sympathy, as does the 'waiting to obey the gong' since the word 'obey' suggests that there is no choice in the matter – a feature of institutional living. Also, that 'boiled eggs', such a pitiful and derisory meal, are the highlight of a Saturday evening further elicits sympathy from the reader. There is much in this verse that contributes to almost all of the themes. Note the repetition of 'waiting' throughout the verse, but especially in the last line, where it is the first and last word. Indeed, it forms the first word of lines 2, 4 and 5, thereby highlighting its significance. Note how the meaning of the word changes: it begins with waiting for a finite time – till tea time, then waiting for a less quantifiable amount of time – the rain can stop sooner or later, then a much less measurable waiting time, the onset of winter, and finally a waiting time that is unknown – just waiting; for death? The notion of winter, a season that we associate with death, suggests that interpretation. The fact that she is 'waiting for the rain to stop' further suggests sadness, since we associate rain with unhappiness and sorrow (the pathetic fallacy).

It would be an excellent idea to use the above as a template for the poems that you are studying. It would also be very useful for the Scottish poems – as a way of setting out themes, textual references and techniques. Once done, it becomes an excellent *aide memoire* (reminder) to use just before the exam.

Now let's try writing a critical essay.

The critical essay is a formal piece of writing: you have to present an argument or line of thought concerning an issue presented to you in the critical essay question.

Let's go through the various stages needed to write a critical essay. Have a look again at the annotated version of the poem, *Waiting Room*, set out above. In *Waiting Room*, we detected the following themes: old age, waiting, change, institutional existence, loneliness, isolation, sympathy. It is also a poem which presents character.

> **Important point !**
>
> Avoid all informalities – such as abbreviations and/ or contractions: no *isn't, wasn't, doesn't, can't, shan't.* Be formal at all times.

We shall answer the following question:

> **Q** Choose a poem which explores one of the following feelings: joy, isolation, loss, sympathy, sadness.
> Discuss how the poet's exploration of the feeling has deepened your understanding of it.

It is always best to plan your answer. Invariably, those candidates who make a plan, however brief, score higher marks than those who launch into the answer.

Plan your answer carefully so that you demonstrate (a) knowledge and understanding of your chosen poem; (b) a relevant analysis of the poem; (c) a relevant evaluation of the text.

Note carefully that although you are being asked to perform two tasks – (i) how the poet explores the feeling, and (ii) how your understanding of the feeling has been deepened – nevertheless the more able candidate will deal with these two aspects together. You'll see when we come to write the essay.

We'll assume that you decide to use *Waiting Room* and you choose to write about the feeling of sadness. Make a brief plan of the essay, notes to keep you relevant and in case you forget something as you write.

> **Important point !**
>
> Introduce your material effectively and concisely *using the wording of the question* so that the marker knows instantly and unambiguously that what you write is relevant; include your agenda.

You know that you want to involve at least two of structure, word choice, imagery, and linguistic features, such as sentence structure.

Let's begin the essay, stage by stage:

(a) Always begin your answer with the words of the question to establish relevance.

'Waiting Room' by Moira Andrew is a poem about an eighty-year-old lady, who is spending her later years in a nursing home. Andrew, by means of a number of poetic and linguistic techniques, creates and explores an atmosphere of sadness surrounding the old lady.

(b) Next, make clear that you are going to deal with structure, word choice, imagery and linguistic features – but under no circumstance write 'I'm going to deal with …': in an English literature answer that sounds too mechanistic and unsophisticated. By stating the techniques that you are going to deal with, you are setting your 'agenda' for the essay. The examiner will then know what to expect. You should write something along the following lines:

Moira Andrew portrays the theme of old age and creates the effects of sympathy and sadness by means of a number of techniques such as structure, word choice, imagery and her deployment of linguistic features.

(continued)

(c) Now you need to take each of these techniques and deal with them in turn. Take structure:

The poem is structured in five verses, each five lines in length. There is no rhyme scheme, nor is the rhythm regular, thus creating a sound very like prose. Such a structure not only makes the poem more accessible for the reader but it also helps reinforce the reflective, rather sad mood of the poem. The first four verses, with the exception of verse 3, begin with the words 'She waits …', thus drawing attention to the fact that the old lady now spends her days waiting. The first stanza states that 'She waits neatly', a comment on her appearance, whereas the second stanza begins with 'She waits graciously', drawing attention more to her demeanour and character, thus helping to engage the sympathy of the reader for the rather sad image thus created. In the fourth stanza, the words 'She waits defiantly' introduce the idea that this old lady, more than 80 years of age, nevertheless has a strength of character and resilience to be admired, thus further engaging the reader's sympathy. Although elderly and clearly infirm – 'the stick a third leg' – nevertheless she doesn't give in to her situation and remains determined and strong-minded, characteristics which we can admire while realising the sadness with which she is surrounded.

But there is more to the structure than the use of anaphora 'She waited + adverb' at the beginning of three verses. The poet also uses the device of enjambement, where the sentence structure takes precedence over the line structure. For example, in verse 2, she writes:

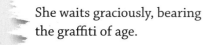

She waits graciously, bearing
the graffiti of age.

The enjambement is created by the use of the caesura after 'graciously', thus causing the sentence to 'spill over' onto the next line. But since the lines still exist, we naturally pause after 'bearing' causing the beginning of the next line to come as a surprise: and the word 'graffiti' certainly surprises us. It's not a word that we associate with old ladies, and when we read it within the context of these two lines we realise the cruelty of age in vandalising the woman's appearance, yet because she 'bear(s) / the graffiti of age', we recognise and feel sadness for the woman's stoical attitude.

Enjambement is used in the middle three verses but not in the first or the last verse. The effect in these two verses is to make each line stand out, one line building on top of the previous one, creating a kind of climax. For example, in the last verse, the fact that the family leaves her is sad enough, but the pile-up of each of the lines following the word 'waiting' creates the final climax of 'waiting for winter, waiting', where the alliteration and the final 'waiting' emphasise the word and help create the suggestion of death.

Another structural device that creates a feeling of sadness is Andrew's use of sentence structure in the final two lines of the third verse:

> Tormented
> she tries to trap them in her tongue

There are two points to be made about the positioning of the word 'Tormented': it's at the beginning of the sentence and it's at the end of the line, both of which places draw attention to the difficulties and frustrations she has in trying to remember names. Also, the poetic devices of alliteration and positioning of the 't' and 'r' sounds further capture the effects of her trying to vocalise names, evoking the reader's feeling of sadness for the annoyance felt by the old lady.

(d) Since the essay isn't quite long enough, we can add perhaps a relevant comment about word choice, as long as we demonstrate by reference to the text how the feature contributes to the feeling of sadness. But be careful, there aren't very many words left! The last verse is particularly sad, especially where the persona explains the old lady is 'waiting to obey the gong'. It would therefore be apposite to write:

Moreover, Andrew also uses word choice to make clear the sadness of the old lady's

Important point

Avoid the formula *quotation + comment* – above all, avoid the formula *quotation, this shows that* ... Work all quotations into the very structure of your sentence – e.g.: 'The first stanza of 'Waiting Room' states that 'She waited neatly', a comment on her appearance, whereas the second stanza begins with 'She waited graciously', drawing attention more to her demeanour and character, thus helping to portray the sadness created by the fact that the woman maintains her dignity in such circumstances'.

(continued)

circumstances in the nursing home, especially when she explains that she has to wait 'to obey the gong' for Saturday tea. The word choice 'obey' conveys more than the lady's lack of choice: she has to comply with the rules of institutional existence – and has to wait to do so. The following parenthetical comment that it is boiled eggs for tea further contributes to the sadness of institutional existence for the elderly – the highlight of the Saturday meal is the parsimony of some boiled eggs. We can infer that there is an assumption that boiled eggs are sufficient for old people of a Saturday evening.

(e) Finally, you have to draw your essay to a conclusion. Sum up the points that you have made without introducing any new material, but do signal clearly to the marker that you are summing up:

Thus it can be seen that by her use of structure, including sentence structure and verse structure, Moira Andrew is able not only to establish a feeling of sadness for the old lady waiting in the nursing home but can, at the same time, explore its significance for the reader.

The essay is around 850 words in length – not that you should waste time counting the words. With practice – and practice is essential when it comes to writing critical essays – you'll be able to gauge what is a sufficient length. But note (a) the formality of the writing; and (b) the ways in which quotations have been incorporated into sentence structure. For longer quotations, though, you can isolate them in lines of their own, as long as they are in both cases woven into the fabric of your argument.

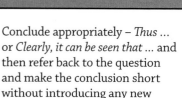

Important point

Make sure that paragraphs are linked as well as your ideas – use transitional terms such as *moreover, furthermore, however,* as well as terms to ensure balance of ideas – on *the one hand … on the other, not only … but also, although x is the case, y also is the case …, nevertheless … accordingly …*

Important point

Conclude appropriately – *Thus …* or *Clearly, it can be seen that …* and then refer back to the question and make the conclusion short without introducing any new material.

Important point

Read carefully what you have written and make corrections – this is a very important part of the exercise since you will pick up poor linkage, any informalities in style or any of the other *don'ts* listed above!

Section 3: The portfolio

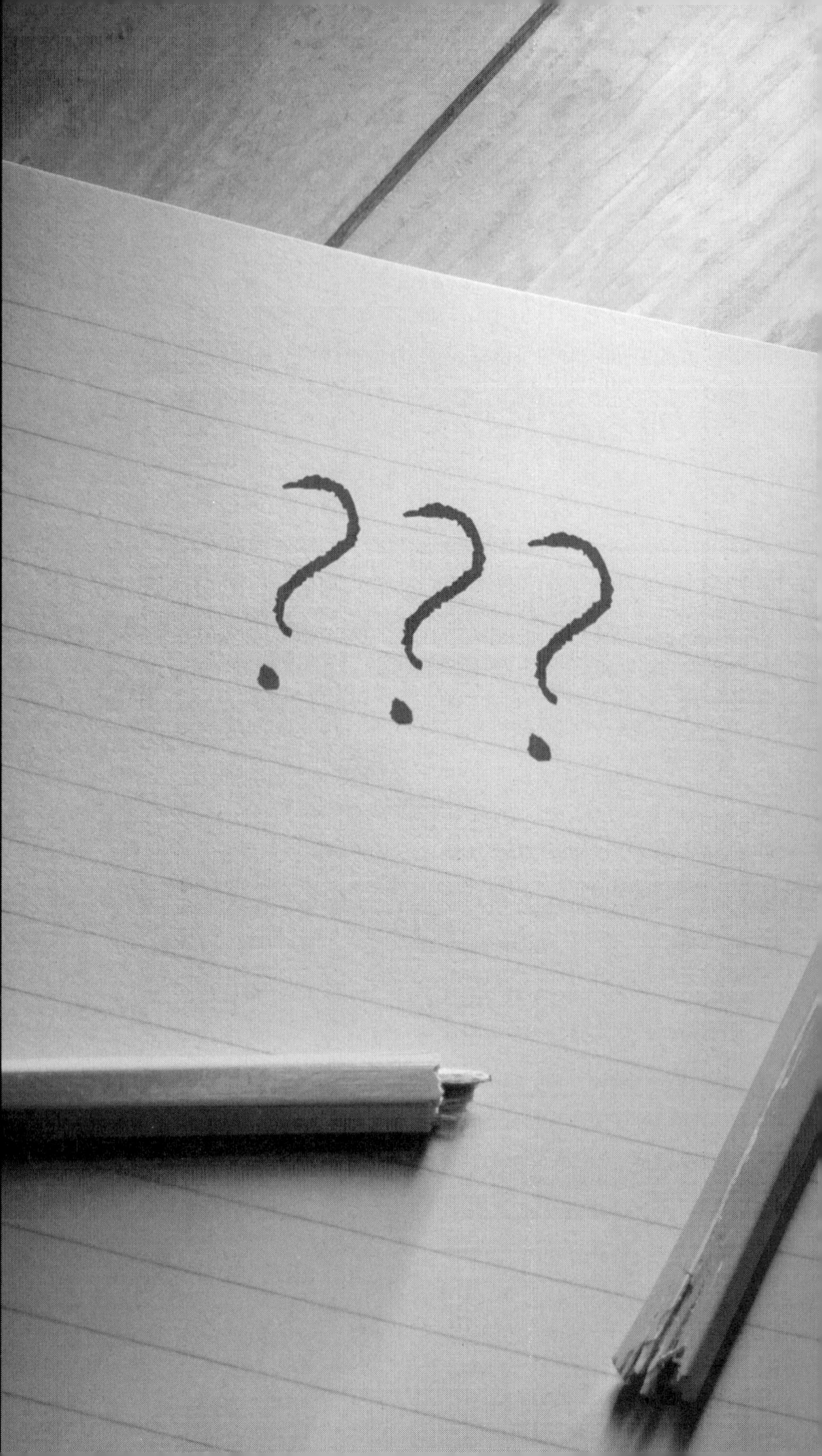

SECTION 3

The portfolio

In Higher English, the writing folio and the critical essay are the two parts where your writing skills are assessed. The writing folio assesses a variety of skills, whereas the critical essay, among other things, assesses your ability to write formally.

Writing – externally assessed portfolio

You know from the introduction to this book that your portfolio of written work has to comprise two written texts that address the main language purposes: discursive writing and writing creatively. Each piece of writing is worth 15 marks, which means that this assessment is worth a considerable 30% of the overall marks for Higher English: it is, therefore, in your interests to produce the best portfolio that you can.

Your portfolio must consist of two pieces of writing of your own choice and each piece, unless you choose to produce poetry, should be no more than 1300 words in length. One piece of writing should be broadly discursive and one piece broadly creative, as set out in the following groups:

Group A: broadly creative

- a personal essay
- a reflective essay
- an imaginative piece

Group B: broadly discursive

- an argumentative essay
- a persuasive essay
- a report for a specified purpose

Before we look at what each of these kinds of writing demands, it is important to recall what you have learned throughout this book: reading and writing are remarkably closely related. The more you develop your reading skills and recognise the various linguistic and literary devices used by skilled authors, the more you will be able to incorporate these same devices into your own writing. Moreover, your writing also improves because you have absorbed at a subconscious, almost subliminal level, many of the techniques used by accomplished writers.

But before you begin your writing, you must consider the **four aspects of writing**:

Purpose – what is it that you are trying to say or achieve?
Structure – what is the most effective way of saying it?
Reader – who is going to read your piece?
Register – given all the above, what is the most effective and appropriate writing style?

First of all, purpose: is your essay to be discursive, persuasive, argumentative, personal/reflective, creative/imaginative? Then you have to work out the structure of the piece: a discursive essay on endangered species of animals will inevitably have a different structure from a short story about unrequited love. Next, you have to decide who your reader is – in this case, most likely your teacher or the examiner at SQA. The structure of your writing and the intended reader will enable you to determine the appropriate register – formal or informal, carefully researched or anecdotal?

It is worth having in mind an actual reader, someone you know will appreciate what you have to say – an uncle, an aunt, a cousin, a friend, your teacher. Write *to* that person, keeping him or her in mind the whole time. Such a method will help keep your writing relevant and focused.

Let's take a simple example of what is meant by these four aspects of writing. You are on holiday and you decide to eschew (shun) text messages and go traditional by sending a postcard to your best friend. The second that you make that decision you have determined the **purpose** of your writing – to tell your friend how much you are enjoying the sea, sand and sun. Also, the fact that it is a postcard determines the **structure** – it has to be short. The **reader** is obvious – your best friend, and he or she as reader will also establish the **register** – a style that is informal and chatty (though your subtext may well be intended to arouse jealousy!).

The various types of writing for the portfolio

Let's take a close look at each of the types of writing outlined above:

Group A

- a personal essay
- a reflective essay
- an imaginative piece

Personal/reflective essay

Many candidates are most comfortable with the personal essay, partly because they think that it is the most straightforward to produce, but what you have to ensure is that your piece is more than the retelling of an experience – you have to display the ability to reflect on the experience.

Furthermore, don't try to produce some great dramatic event; use a fairly simple experience, but give plenty of personal detail in such a way that you imply the effect that it had on you. You should also consider symbolism to represent some of the aspects of the experience about which you are writing. Think about the pathetic fallacy, but don't overdo it.

Whatever, avoid producing a rambling, witless anecdote. There is nothing more boring than a story that has neither wit nor point: give your story shape and ensure that it is reflective and, above all, interesting.

Imaginative essay

Normally we think of a short story when we think of creative writing, but your essay need not be restricted to the short story format – you can produce a piece of prose fiction which is an extract from a novel. You can produce a poem or a dramatic script, such as a monologue, a short scene, or a sketch. If you decide to produce a short story, try not to choose a subject about which you know nothing. And do remember the format of the short story: few characters, a simple plot, best based on your own experience and a resolution which will make the reader think – or, at least, smile!

Group B

- an argumentative essay
- a persuasive essay
- a report for a specified purpose

Discursive/argumentative essay

Most people think that this is the most difficult type of writing and, while it is not easy, you have to remember that you have to produce – under exam conditions – a discursive essay: that is, your critical essay!

The essay you produce for the critical essay is discursive in that you are presenting an argument or line of thought. Since a discursive essay is an essay where you set out an argument, you have to master the skills of marshalling ideas and thoughts, presenting them in a logical sequence and then expressing them in precise, formal prose.

In your discursive essay, try to steer away from clichéd topics such as animal rights, or euthanasia, or media celebrities, unless you present such subjects from an original, stimulating angle. Better still, write about something that really engages you and about which you can engage your reader's interest. Try to deal with subjects that are as appealing as they are current: pay attention to the press, to the news and even to issues being dealt with in TV serial dramas for contemporary, polemical issues and controversial disputes.

Persuasive essay

Persuasive writing is not unlike discursive writing in that you choose a subject about which you feel very strongly, though, unlike discursive writing, you do not need to present a carefully constructed argument. Nor do you need to take account of counter arguments. You do need, however, to use the language of persuasion to coax, or even cajole, your reader to your point of view. For those of you already skilled with language, the persuasive essay could be an excellent choice.

Report essay

Although many of you may not even consider report writing for your portfolio, you should think again. After you leave school/university, and are in employment at last, the type of writing that you will be most asked to produce will be report writing. First of all, find the right material: choose a topic about which opinions are divided. Research your material from newspapers, books, the Internet, but ensure that you have a balance of opinion. Reorganise the material into a coherent piece of continuous formal prose of an appropriate length.

Remember: (a) to produce a careful, concise, effective introduction, because your reader will not have read the source material; (b) to develop your ideas relevantly and coherently – the test of a good report is coherence (does it read well and hang together?) and the extent to which the report achieves balance; (c) to be sure to conclude your report with an ending that sums up what you have said, but contains no new ideas. Make sure that your report is cohesive – that your line of thought is logical, but balanced, and that your paragraphs are effectively linked.

Especially in argumentative and report writing – and in your critical essay – learn to use transition phrases, such as 'in order to', 'for example', 'unfortunately', 'moreover', 'furthermore', 'as a result', 'on the one hand … on the other hand'. Such phrases, used appropriately, help to create linkage and cohesion in your writing.

What the SQA is looking for

For broadly creative writing, the SQA is looking for, at best, an essay where dedicated attention has been paid to the four aspects of writing, an essay (a) which shows a real command of creative writing, (b) where issues and themes have been established and developed, and (c) where experiences that reveal considered ideas and feelings have been explored in a mature and self-reflective way. The essay should show maturity and sensitivity, but, even more, it should reveal a real sense of the writer's personality and individual style. It also has to show the writer's skill in using structure, language and other devices to shape meaning and effect with confident and varied expression.

For broadly discursive writing, the SQA is looking for most of the above, along with evidence that the writer has made appropriate selection from considerable research into the chosen topic and at the same time has demonstrated skill in establishing and maintaining a clearly developed line of thought. The essay also has to show the writer's skill in using structure, language and other devices to shape meaning and convey depth and complexity of thought with confident and varied expression. The essay must show an ability to present an argument convincingly and persuasively, if appropriate.

The above requirements are for top essays. To help you achieve such marks, pay attention to the following advice.

Ways to improve your writing

When you start writing, reflect on all that you have learned in the language section of this book: have a look again at all the language techniques that we have analysed in the RUAE section. Make sure that you adopt the appropriate register for your piece; vary your sentence structure and vocabulary; use lists, especially tricolon, some with built-in contrasts; experiment with striking non-clichéd imagery, especially metaphor, simile and personification; and, most importantly, introduce and conclude the essay aptly. Think of all the other devices with which you are now familiar: foreshadowing, symbolism, the pathetic fallacy (use of weather to suggest mood and/or emotion).

Use of inversion

Whatever the piece you choose to write, keep the four aspects of writing firmly in mind – now and in later life. Pay very close attention to sentence structure. You could, for example, use **inversion** and place a prepositional phrase at the beginning of a sentence instead of the usual place, at the end. For example:

> The eagle was released into the wild on the thirtieth of November as the sun broke through the clouds.

There are two prepositional phrases in that sentence: *on the thirtieth of November* and *as the sun broke through the clouds*. Let's try altering the positioning of the prepositional phrases:

> As the sun broke through the clouds on the thirtieth of November, the eagle was released into the wild.

Or even:

> On the thirtieth of November, as the sun broke through the clouds, the eagle was released into the wild.

In the first case, because the adverbial clause is at the beginning of the sentence, the main clause 'the eagle was released' is delayed to the end, thus creating climax, thereby drawing attention to their release. In the second case, however, although there is still build-up to the release of the eagle, nevertheless by placing the adverbial phrase 'On the thirtieth of November' at the very beginning, attention is being drawn to the date as well – suggesting that the date of the eagle's release is significant: St Andrew's Day.

In both cases, the sentences actually sound more interesting. Remember this in your own writing: variety of structure by re-positioning phrases or subordinate clauses can be an effective way of arresting the reader's attention! As can be the use of lists (especially tricolon), parallel structure (anaphora) and climax.

But bear in mind that the positioning of subordinate clauses at the beginning of sentences can be a marker of formal English – and that is important to remember when it comes to discursive writing, which must be in a formal register!

Look at the following sentence, taken from the essay *Why I Write* by George Orwell. He is outlining his motivation for writing discursive prose:

> When I sit down to write a book, I do not say to myself 'I am going to produce a work of art'. I write it because there is some lie that I want to expose, some fact to which I want to draw attention, and my initial concern is to get a hearing.

Note the subordinate clause at the beginning of the sentence: 'When I sit down to write a book', a clause which is actually an essential context for the rest of the sentence – it makes sense of 'I do not say to myself "I am going to produce a work of art."' But it also provides variety in his sentence structure.

Note also his use of tricolon – always an effective structure – in the next sentence, as well as the use of anaphora (parallel structure): 'I write' + 'some lie that', 'I want' + 'some fact to which' leading to the climactic 'my initial concern is to get a hearing'. The rhythm created by this structure is particularly effective in creating the climax – all techniques that you would do well to adopt and incorporate into your own writing.

All these are techniques to use in your own writing in order to give it variety and style.

Use of short and long sentences

The use of short and long sentences is another technique by which you can add variety to your prose and also create dramatic impact.

Look at these sentences from *Regeneration* by Pat Barker. The novel is set in 1917, in Edinburgh, at Craiglockhart, a place where shell-shocked soldiers were sent to recuperate from the trench warfare of the First World War. In one scene, a character, Burns, is standing by the window of his room, thinking about taking a bus out of Edinburgh to escape for a while:

> A sharp gust of wind blew rain against the glass. Somehow or other he was going to have to get out. It wasn't forbidden, it was even encouraged, though he himself didn't go out much. He got his coat and went downstairs. On the corridor he met one of the nurses from his ward, who looked surprised to see him wearing his coat, but didn't ask where he was going.
>
> At the main gates he stopped. Because he'd been inside so long, the possibilities seemed endless, though they resolved themselves quickly into two. Into Edinburgh, or away. And that was no choice at all: he knew he wasn't up to facing traffic.

Look at the number of short sentences: they add dramatic impact beside the longer ones, especially before the long final sentence of the first paragraph. Also interesting is the short sentence at the beginning of the second paragraph, again contrasting with the long last sentence of the previous paragraph. It not only creates drama, but it also creates pace – the short sentences convey the man's panic to the reader. Note also the dramatic effect of the sentence beginning with 'And', the effect of which is to isolate and dramatise the point being made in that sentence.

Look at this next example, where a sentence begins in an unusual way. It is from an article in *The Guardian* by Alistair Cooke. He had been describing the extreme care taken by Wells Fargo, a security company, when collecting vast sums of money from various organisations to take to the bank. These are his final two paragraphs:

Important point !

For some reason, we are taught in our early years never to begin a sentence with 'And', yet that can be a very effective way of beginning a sentence, especially a final one, as is the case here.

The money bags are marked and carried by the security men to a guard who was locked in the truck on its arrival. The guard signals that all is well to the driver, who climbs aboard, pausing only to check his sidearms. The truck takes off on the long drive to Wall Street, where the bags are lifted across the sidewalk under the watchful eye of the armed truck crew and two receiving guards, alerted by an electronic buzz as soon as the truck stops outside.

In fact, you could say that the only time the money bags are flashed in public is on their brief passage across the sidewalk in front of the Morgan Guaranty Trust Co. at 23 Wall Street. Which was where, last Wednesday, three agile young men grabbed them and made off with a total swag of one million, three hundred and seventy-seven thousand dollars.

Look at the final sentence. It begins with a relative pronoun – Which – and that is most unusual because a relative pronoun agrees with its antecedent – in this case, '23 Wall Street'. But the effect is comic, especially with the insertion of the phrases 'last Wednesday' and 'three agile young men grabbed them and made off' which has the effect once again of climax: the joke is delayed until the very end of the sentence. Note also that $1,377,000 is written in words, which also makes the joke more effective because that way it makes the amount seem so much more.

Link sentences

Another important aspect of all writing is to ensure that your piece is cohesive: ensure, therefore, that the paragraphs are linked in such a way that the piece 'hangs together' as one unit. Note in the above example that Alistair Cooke uses 'In fact' to link the paragraphs.

Link sentences are especially important in discursive, formal writing since they enable the line of thought to flow more easily, thus allowing the argument to be developed effectively.

Use of colon and semi-colon

As we have already noted, the semi-colon, especially, is an underused, underrated punctuation mark. Not only does its use make your writing appear stylish, it is actually very helpful in indicating a connection between two units of sense. Often, you can avoid the comma splice by using the semi-colon.

The colon is useful for the introduction of lists and explanations. Again, it is a stylish punctuation mark.

Use of imagery, tone, word choice

The problem with much writing is that very often it is clichéd: the writer uses tired, worn-out metaphors that we have all heard too often before. Try to use original expressions, original images. Laurie Lee, in *Cider with Rosie*, describes two friends as 'limpet chums', a vividly original and therefore effective expression which captures perfectly their closeness both emotionally and physically – clearly, it was almost impossible to prise the chums apart!

Look at the following extract from Clive James's book, *The Crystal Bucket*, a collection of pieces from his time as a television columnist for *The Observer* newspaper. In the excerpt below, James considers the impact made on the viewer by the original series of *The Incredible Hulk*:

Hulk has a standard body-builder's physique, with two sets of shoulders one on top of the other and wings of lateral muscle that hold his arms out from his sides as if his armpits had piles. He is made remarkable by his avocado complexion, eyes like plovers' eggs and the same permanently exposed lower teeth displayed by Richard Harris[1] when he is acting determined, or indeed just acting.

Given a flying start by the shock effect of his personal appearance, Hulk goes into action against the heavies, flinging them about in slow motion. Like Bionic Woman, Six Million Dollar Man and Wonderwoman, Hulk does his action numbers at glacial speed. Emitting slow roars of rage, Hulk runs very slowly towards the enemy, who slowly attempt to make their escape. But no matter how slowly they run, Hulk runs more slowly. Slowly he picks them up, gradually bangs their head together, and with a supreme burst of lethargy throws them through the side of a building.

[1]Richard Harris – an actor famous in the 1970s and '80s and more recently in the Harry Potter films.

The paragraphs sparkle with originality. There is running throughout a gentle sarcasm mocking the programme. Expressions such as: 'two sets of shoulders one on top of the other and wings of lateral muscle that hold his arms out from his sides as if his armpits had piles' contribute to the sarcastic tone because they create such ridiculous images – the juxtaposition of armpits and piles, for example, is as witty as it is outrageous. Clive James is using the language to create original witticisms, avoiding clichés and worn-out jokes. The expression, 'Hulk does his action numbers at glacial speed', is particularly effective because 'glacial speed' is an oxymoron: glaciers, however they may move, do not move at speed! Yet the image captures so accurately television's obsession (still there to this day) with using slow motion to portray violent action that could only in reality take place quickly.

The repetition of the notion of slowness in the last paragraph is highly effective because James does not just repeat the word 'slowly' but develops the idea with words such as 'gradually' and 'lethargy', the latter made all the more effective by the oxymoron – 'supreme burst of lethargy'. The word 'burst', intensified by the superlative 'supreme', meaning extremely intense, maximum possible, suggests a sudden, forceful explosion, which contradicts the idea of 'lethargy' with its suggestion of sluggishness and listlessness. It's an original and effective way of drawing attention to meaning.

Rule: avoid at all costs clichéd writing and image fatigue; instead look for highly original and arresting images that will intensify what you want to say. A good idea is to note from your own reading – books, magazines, newspaper articles – any striking images that you could adapt for your own purposes.

Sometimes it can be very effective to take a well-known saying, adage, proverb or aphorism and subvert it (stand it on its head): for example, Jill Tweedie's 'every silver lining has its cloud'; Oscar Wilde's 'Divorces are made in Heaven'; 'The truth is rarely pure and never simple'.

Use of subversion

It can also be very interesting to subvert a well-known story: search for Roald Dahl's poem 'Goldilocks', for example: he turns the story of Goldilocks and the three bears on its head to surprising and witty effect. Also, Angela Carter subverts the Little Red Riding Hood story in 'The Bloody Chamber', a book of her Gothic short stories. You could try subverting a well-known folk story or fairy tale to change the moral or the outcome, giving it a 21st century relevance.

Conclusion

I hope that this book has taught you a great deal about words, sentence structure, punctuation, paragraphs, paragraph linkage, narrative structure, imagery and other literary devices. I also hope that not only will you avoid solecisms in your written English but that your prose style will vibrate – nay, coruscate – with original and apt imagery.

But I also hope I have gone further than dealing with technique alone. The technicalities of language are only the methods by which meaning is expressed: after all, alter the form of a sentence and you alter its meaning. Remember?

But it is not only sentences that have meaning. All literature is invested with meaning – themes, issues, areas of experience to be investigated and explored. Even *Coronation Street* portrays issues that affect us either socially or personally, no doubt informing some aspect of human relationships. How much more, then, does *Hamlet* or *The Crucible* or *My Last Duchess* comment on and interpret our experience? And the process is two-way: we have to take our experiences to the text in order to make sense of it and, at the same time, our experience is thereby heightened and illuminated and our understanding enlightened and enhanced.

I trust that this book has helped you improve your reading skills and that you regard all literature as something more than a task to be endured in order to pass exams. Literature is not like some geometric theorem that has to be conned by rote and regurgitated at will. Our greatest poets, novelists and dramatists did not really have Higher English in mind when they penned some of the most inspiring masterpieces of all time. Literature is there to be enjoyed, not just for its own sake, though that is important, but for what it tells us about our human condition.